LIVERPOOL: SHAPING THE CITY

RIBA ⌗ Publishing

Liverpool
City Council

© RIBA ENTERPRISES LTD AND LIVERPOOL CITY COUNCIL, 2010

Published by RIBA Publishing
15 Bonhill Street
London EC2P 2EA

ISBN 978 1 85946 329 1
Stock Code 68970

The right of Stephen Bayley to be identified as the Author of this Work
has been asserted in accordance with the Copyright, Designs and
Patents Act 1988 Sections 77 and 78.

British Library Cataloguing-in-Publication Data
A catalogue record for this book is available from the British Library.

Publisher: Steven Cross
Commissioning Editor: Lucy Harbor
Project Editor: Susan George
Written by: Stephen Bayley
Photo Editor: Paul McMullin
Copy Editor: Ian McDonald
Designed by Kneath Associates
Printed and bound by Butler Tanner & Dennis Ltd, Frome and London

RIBA Publishing is part of RIBA Enterprises Ltd.
www.ribaenterprises.com

i

Front Cover Image: The waterfront, Liverpool
Photographer: Paul McMullin

CONTENTS

LIVERPOOL: SHAPING THE CITY

FOREWORD	1
PREFACE	3
ACKNOWLEDGEMENTS	5
PUBLISHING PARTNERS	7
TIMELINE	13
INTRODUCTION	17
CHAPTER 1	
LIVERPOOL PAST	21
CHAPTER 2	
LIVERPOOL PRESENT	41
CHAPTER 3	
TRANSFORMING THE CITY	55
> Public Realm	58
> A Place to Shop	80
> A Place to Work	98
> A Place to Visit	112
> A Place to Live	140
> A Place to Learn	156
CHAPTER 4	
SHAPING THE FUTURE	173
FURTHER READING	188

FOREWORD

RUTH REED

Royal Institute of British Architects, President 2009–2011

As the President of the RIBA – a position previously held by Sir Giles Gilbert Scott, the architect of the Liverpool Anglican Cathedral, during the centenary year of the institute – it gives me great pleasure to be writing the foreword for a book about a city whose architecture has once again captured the public's imagination.

During my presidency I will be working with members across the country to share best practice and ensure that we retain our world class profession to meet the challenges of the current economic climate. Liverpool has certainly produced its fair share of best practice over the last few years, and in 2009 Liverpool One by BDP became the first masterplan to be nominated for the RIBA Stirling Prize. This should come as no surprise to a city which has a history of 'firsts'. Amongst its architectural and engineering achievements, Liverpool boasts the first building which used skyscraper technology, the first commercial wet dock and the world's first hydraulic cargo-handling systems.

This inventiveness is just one aspect of the history of a city rich in architectural heritage. When you consider its size, Liverpool has a disproportionately high number of listed buildings, and the view of the waterfront skyline reveals just how many iconic buildings the city holds.

The announcement in 2003 that Liverpool would be European Capital of Culture in 2008 was undoubtedly a catalyst for the surge in regeneration projects within the city centre over the last few years. The RIBA hosted two events in the city during that year – the RIBA Stirling Prize dinner took place at the critically acclaimed Arena and Convention Centre designed by Wilkinson Eyre Architects, and the Le Corbusier exhibition visited the crypt of the Liverpool Metropolitan Cathedral, designed by Sir Edwin Lutyens. The exhibition would not have been possible without the huge support from local practices, many of whom have projects which are featured in this book.

Liverpool has been successful in transforming the city centre into a place where people can once again enjoy working, shopping, visiting or simply relaxing in public spaces. The challenge for the next decade will be for the great architecture and urban design achieved in the centre to reach some of the suburbs where regeneration is desperately needed.

< Moonrise over Liverpool
PAUL MCMULLIN

PREFACE

COUNCILLOR WARREN BRADLEY

Leader of Liverpool City Council

I'm enormously proud to be the Leader of Liverpool City Council, especially at this time in the city's history when it is emerging from a long decline and once again is being described with superlatives. For many outside the city, the stereotypical image of Liverpool is of a denuded and struggling place, and this has been informed by questionable media coverage that begins and ends with clichés rather than realities.

But Liverpool is a World Heritage Site, with one of the most recognisable waterfronts in the world. Its collection of historic buildings is one of the finest and most spectacular in England. Culturally the city punches well above its weight, with more galleries and museums per capita than anywhere in the UK, and with a Biennial that grows from strength to strength. Even in the darkest days these historic buildings were here, witnesses to a fall from grace perhaps, but nevertheless powerful guardians of Liverpool's past prowess and the inevitable return to former glories.

It seems that these treasures have only been rediscovered and appreciated by others in recent years, as Liverpool has surged ahead with regeneration projects. Ironically it has taken a whole series of new buildings and public realm schemes to thrust the city back into the spotlight. And this time for all the right reasons. Liverpool has one of the fastest growing economies in the UK, its successful 2008 Capital of Culture celebrations are recognised as a model of good practice, it is the UK's third most popular visitor destination and it has risen into the top five retail cities.

The buildings and spaces in this book demonstrate that the city not only understands the importance of respecting its heritage, but also how to add to this unique legacy, producing contemporary buildings and spaces that are dynamic, exciting and informed. I would like to take this opportunity to thank the public and private sectors for working together to deliver this 'new' Liverpool, a phenomenal joint effort that demonstrates a massive commitment to and confidence in the future of this city. There is still much to be done, and there is no room for complacency, but I am confident that the strategies being put in place now will lead to further transformational work.

The buildings illustrated here show that Liverpool knows what it means to strive for world-class architecture and urban design, and I would like to thank the RIBA for show-casing the city. If you don't mind me saying – its about time.

< Liver Building as seen from Martins Bank
PAUL MCMULLIN

v Cyclist riding over Bascule Bridge, Stanley Dock
MATTHEW DILLON

v The Liverpool skyline
PAUL MCMULLIN

ACKNOWLEDGEMENTS

I would like to thank the members of the editorial team who have been involved from the outset, and without whom this book would not have been possible. Thanks to Nigel Lee of Liverpool City Council, and Jenny Douglas and Peter Smith at Liverpool Vision for their enthusiasm, hard work and not least their sense of humour that made for very entertaining editorial team meetings. And in particular I am extremely grateful to Rob Burns of the City Council who deserves a special thank you for all the help he has given to pull together the case study chapters. Credit must also be given to Collum Giles and his colleagues at English Heritage who have provided constructive advice on the drafts of the book.

Paul McMullin, the photo editor for the book, has provided the majority of the stunning images which illustrate this book, and many have been specially photographed. Many thanks to all those who have contributed to the case study chapter. John Stonard of Design Liverpool has provided invaluable support throughout, and Belinda Irlam-Mowbray and Dominic Wilkinson kindly gave up time to help select the case studies for the book. I must also thank all the contributors to the future vision chapter who have not already had a mention – Michael Parkinson, Paul Monaghan and John Kelly.

Finally I would like to thank the author of the first two chapters, Stephen Bayley, for writing a thoroughly entertaining critique of Liverpool, and one which, fortunately for us, was slightly less controversial than his last book which was published at the end of 2009.

Lucy Harbor

Commissioning Editor

< View from Albert Dock towards Liverpool One
PAUL MCMULLIN

PUBLISHING PARTNERS

We would like to thank all of the companies listed here who have generously supported the publication of this wonderful book.

The development and regeneration of Liverpool is a success story for all those involved – from those working within the City Council, Liverpool Vision, the investors, developers, architects, contractors, organisations such as the Homes and Communities Agency and English Heritage, to, ultimately, the local businesses, people and communities.

None of what you will see and read in this book could have been achieved without the support and encouragement of companies like those listed here. We thank them for their support and look forward to working with them in the future.

Ruth Reed and Councillor Warren Bradley

DESIGNLIVERPOOL

DESIGN**LIVERPOOL**

DESIGN LIVERPOOL

Design Liverpool is a partnership between the Commission for Architecture and the Built Environment (CABE), Liverpool City Council and the Northwest Regional Development Agency represented through Places Matter. The initiative was developed to explore how national objectives for promoting excellence in the built environment can be promoted at a local level. With a coordinated programme of advocacy, skills development, enabling and public engagement, Design Liverpool aims to engage with a broad range of audiences and help make the creation of high quality places a common objective.

www.designliverpool.org.uk

ENGLISH HERITAGE

ENGLISH HERITAGE

English Heritage is probably best known for the historic sites in our care which are open to the public. Less well known is our role in looking after the historic environment as a whole, including historic buildings, monuments and areas, and archaeological remains. We aim not only to ensure the preservation of our historic surroundings for the future, but also to encourage people to appreciate and enjoy this heritage today.

www.english-heritage.org.uk

∨ Egerton Street Housing
JOHN STONARD

∨ Mersey Ferry and Echo Arena and Conference Centre
PAUL MCMULLIN

 Homes &
Communities
Agency

 Liverpool
City Council

THE HOMES AND COMMUNITIES AGENCY

The Homes and Communities Agency (HCA) is the single, national housing and regeneration agency for England. Its role is to create opportunities for people to live in high quality, sustainable places. It provides funding for affordable housing, brings land back into productive use and improves quality of life by raising standards for the physical and social environment.

Working with partners, the HCA is a landowner, key influencer and major investor in regeneration activity across Liverpool, including a number of major high profile schemes, such as Kings Waterfront, Lime Street Gateway and Edge Lane. The HCA is also investing heavily in housing market renewal and development across the city.

www.homesandcommunities.co.uk

LIVERPOOL CITY COUNCIL

Liverpool City Council is the largest local authority in Merseyside and has overseen a transformation in the city in the last two decades. The City Council has attracted significant investment, worked with key public sector partners such as Liverpool Vision, the Northwest Regional Development Agency and the Homes and Communities Agency. The city has also formed strong relationships with the private sector – a key factor in the regeneration of the city centre – including national organisations such as Grosvenor, and local businesses such as Neptune and Downing Developments.

Creativity and a passion for Liverpool at all levels has led to major accolades for the city, including European Capital of Culture 2008, and World Heritage Site status in 2004, and in 2010 Liverpool will be the only British city to have its own pavilion at the Shanghai Expo.

www.liverpool.gov.uk

ˇ Victoria Building and Museum
PAUL MCMULLIN

ˇ St George's Hall
PAUL MCMULLIN

LIVERPOOL JOHN MOORES UNIVERSITY

Liverpool John Moores University encompasses the ethos of the Littlewoods' Pools founder it is named after as an innovative and forward-thinking university. It is one of Britain's largest universities with approximately 24,000 students. Strengths include sport and exercise sciences, physics, astronomy, computer science and informatics, electrical and electronic engineering, architecture and built environment, anthropology, biological sciences and general engineering. It is a Centre for Excellence in teaching and learning in sport, exercise, dance and physical activity, and is the only university in the Northwest to be awarded Skillset Media Academy status. A £180 million building programme to be concluded by 2013 includes an Art and Design Academy and Life Sciences building housing the Schools of Psychology and Sport and Exercise Sciences.

www.ljmu.ac.uk

LIVERPOOL VISION

Liverpool Vision is the economic development company responsible for the city's physical and economic regeneration. The company has played a key role in the city's positive and dramatic transformation over the past decade and continues to lead its development.

Liverpool has once again become one of the UK's leading business and tourist destinations through an ambitious and far-reaching regeneration programme. In recent years over £4 billion has been committed to physical and economic regeneration.

We have set out a long term vision for Liverpool as a confident and competitive international city, a vibrant knowledge centre and cultural capital where dynamic creativity drives a thriving and inclusive economy – simply one of the best places to live, work, invest and enjoy life.

www.liverpoolvision.co.uk

v Port of Liverpool Building
PAUL MCMULLIN

v John Lennon Airport exterior
PAUL MCMULLIN

NEPTUNE DEVELOPMENTS

Neptune Developments has a distinguished track record of success in the field of property development. Together with Countryside Properties, one of the country's leading quality house builders, they have delivered Mann Island - simply the best in location, quality and value.

Mann Island contrasts with but enhances its historic waterfront setting and is set to become Liverpool's prime location to live, work and play. Situated at the heart of Liverpool's waterfront World Heritage site, this unique development combines cutting edge architectural design, the finest materials, stunning views and superb public realm.

With the support of the NWDA, the building has been developed to the highest standards to reflect the importance of the location and has already become a new landmark for the city.

www.neptunedevelopments.co.uk

UNIVERSITY OF LIVERPOOL

The University of Liverpool is one of the UK's leading research institutions, with a world-class research portfolio and an annual turnover of £364 million, including £130 million for research.

Ranked by *The Financial Times* as the 14th largest research university in the UK and in its Top 10 for research productivity and industrial grant income, the University of Liverpool is a member of the prestigious Russell Group, comprising the 20 leading research universities in the UK.

Associated with nine Nobel Laureates, the University of Liverpool is recognised for its high quality teaching and research. The University has 21,000 students on undergraduate and postgraduate courses, including international and online students from more than 100 countries.

www.liv.ac.uk

TIMELINE

1207 'Liverpool' created by Royal Charter of King John, its position on the peninsula between river and tidal creek making it a convenient harbour for communication with Ireland. Seven medieval streets soon established.

1235 Construction of Liverpool castle.

1548 Estimated population 500-600.

1555 Liverpool has 15 registered ships totalling 222 tons.

1648 First recorded cargo from America arrives: 30 tons of Tobacco, onboard the 'Friendship'.

1660s Merchants displaced from London by the Great Fire and the Great Plague settle in Liverpool.

1667 Sugar refining begins in the West Indies.

1698 Liverpool now has 24 streets, 'mostly new build houses of brick and stone after the London fashion … built high and built even'.

1700 Estimated population 5,000.

1700 'Blessing' was the first recorded slave ship to set sail from Liverpool.

1715 The first commercial enclosed wet dock in the world opens in Liverpool, later known as Old Dock and now conserved beneath Liverpool One.

1718 Bluecoat Chambers completed, showing Wren's influence – the oldest surviving building in the city centre.

1740 Liverpool overtakes Bristol as second port and takes a higher share of the slave trade. Manufactured goods exported by ship to West Africa are traded for enslaved Africans who are trafficked to the West Indies in exchange for cargoes of rum, sugar, tobacco and cotton.

1754 Current Town Hall completed by John Wood of Bath.

1757 Liverpool merchants finance the construction of the Sankey Brook Canal – the nation's first major man-made inland navigation.

1770 Work commences on the Leeds and Liverpool canal, providing a direct connection with the major manufacturing centres of Lancashire and Yorkshire. Completed in 1816, it is the highest and longest in Britain.

1792 Liverpool now handling a sixth of all tonnage from all English ports, compared with one 24th of all tonnage in 1716.

1797 The city booms, but prosperity comes at a price – 'throughout this large built Town every Brick is cemented to its fellow Brick by the blood and sweat of Negros', according to the Rev. William Bagshaw Stevens. The learned Athenaeum Club is founded by William Roscoe and his circle.

1801 Population 77,653.

1807 Abolition of transportation of slaves by British ships assisted by Liverpool MP William Roscoe, but other trade continues to expand.

1816 Leeds and Liverpool Canal completed.

1820 James Wyatt completes remodelling of Town Hall, comparable with London's Mansion House in its richness.

1830 The Liverpool and Manchester Railway opens – the world's first commercial railway to carry passengers, goods and mail.

1836 Opening of Lime Street Station.

∧ Buck's view of Liverpool, 1725
LCC

1837	The first 'grand' steeplechase, later to become the Grand National, is run at Aintree.
1840	The Liverpool Sanitation Act leads to the appointment of Dr Duncan as the country's first City Medical Officer and to James Newlands' pioneering sewer system.
1845	Completion of the Albert Dock.
1850	Liverpool has 1,834 registered ships carrying 514,635 tons.
1851	Population 375,955.
1854	St George's Hall completed.
1864	Completion of Oriel Chambers by Peter Ellis, an early example of curtain wall construction that outraged commentators – 'a kind of greenhouse architecture run mad', *Building News*.
1869	St Martin's Cottages, the first corporation housing in Britain, are opened.
1880	Royal Charter grants Liverpool city status.
1888	Work begins on Lever Brothers' Port Sunlight factory and model village on the Cheshire bank of the Mersey.
1892	Following a dispute over rent for use of the sports ground at Anfield Road, Everton Football Club moves to Goodison Park and Liverpool Football Club is founded.
1893	Opening of the Liverpool Overhead Railway along the waterfront to alleviate docklands traffic congestion – the world's first electric overhead railway.
1895	Britain's first school of architecture and applied art opens in Liverpool.
1901	Population 684,958.
1903	From an all Gothic shortlist, Giles Gilbert Scott wins the competition to design the city's first Anglican cathedral.
1904	Charles Reilly becomes influential head of Liverpool School of Architecture (a post he held until 1933).

1911	The concrete-framed Royal Liver Building by Walter Thomas completed on the Pier Head. Together with the Mersey Docks and Harbour Board Building (1907) and the Cunard Building (1916), it is one of three individual muscular buildings that give the city its distinctive waterfront.
1914–1918	First World War: serious shipping losses.
1929	Viscount Leverhulme establishes the school of Civic Design; the world's first planning school.
1931	Population 855,688.
1933	Roman Catholic Cathedral by Edwin Lutyens begun, with a Brobdingnagian scale and ambition to rival St Peter's in Rome, but only the crypt will ever be completed.
1934	Mersey Road Tunnel opens – the longest underwater road tunnel in the world.
1939	Outbreak of Second World War.
1941	Seven consecutive nights of bombing during the infamous 'May Blitz' kills 4000 people and destroys much of the city centre. Reporting of the extent of damage suppressed due to fears of its affect on morale.
1947	Major Town Planning exhibition showcases proposals for the post-war rebuilding of Liverpool with the 'Shennan Plan' as its centrepiece.
1950s	Post-war rebuilding.
1951	Population 790,838.
1961	City Planning Department established Beatles first appear at the Cavern Club.
1965	The City Council publishes The Shankland Plan – an ambitious framework for the future with proposals for wholesale demolition and redevelopment with pedestrians separated from vehicles via an extensive network of 'high level walkways', one of the earliest pedestrianised schemes in the UK.

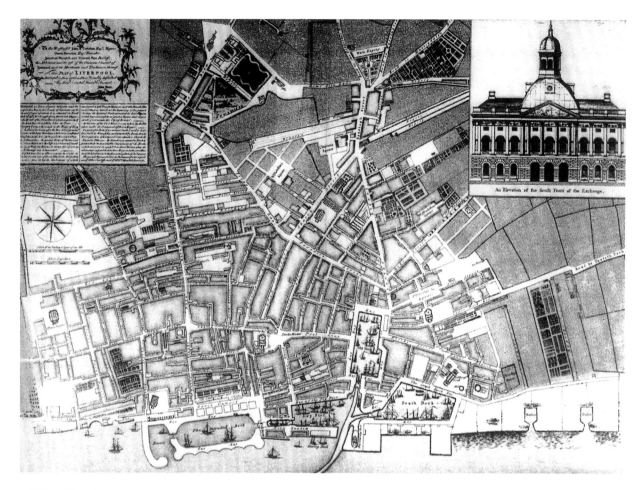

^ 1765 map of Liverpool
LCC

1967	Frederick Gibberd's Metropolitan Cathedral of Christ the King completed, its radical circular form, reflecting Vatican 2, breaks with traditional axial organisation.	**1999**	Liverpool Vision established as the first urban regeneration company in the UK.
1972	The South Docks, including Albert Dock, are abandoned and become silted.	**2001**	Population 439,473.
1978	Completion of Giles Gilbert Scott's Anglican cathedral.	**2003**	Selection of Liverpool as European Capital of Culture 2008.
1981	Toxteth riots. Michael Heseltine appointed as Minister for Merseyside. Merseyside Development Corporation established to deliver regeneration.	**2004**	Liverpool – 'Maritime Mercantile City' inscribed as a World Heritage Site by UNESCO.
1984	Liverpool International Garden Festival.	**2008**	Liverpool is European Capital of Culture.
1988	Tate Liverpool by James Stirling crowns a major redevelopment of Albert Dock, the largest single conservation project ever undertaken in the UK.	**2009**	Leeds and Liverpool Canal link through Pier Head opens, connecting south docks to the national inland waterway network.
1991	Population 449,560.		

INTRODUCTION

People do not feel indifferent to Liverpool. Its drama —
whether you see it as epic, comic or tragic (or perhaps a bit
of each) — requires strong responses. And it gets them.

A depressing little poem by Paul Birtill was published in
The Spectator on 27 September 2008. But, then, this is
a magazine with some history of slighting the glorious, but
exasperating, capital of Merseyside.

^ Princes Road Synagogue
PAUL MCMULLIN

In 2004, Boris Johnson, now Mayor of London (at the time, editor of *The Spectator* and a Conservative MP), accused Liverpudlians of being whining recidivists and wallowing in their 'victim status' – what with record unemployment, a broken economic compass, epic social problems and an uncertain future. This hyperbole caused an entirely predictable outcry, which was, one imagines, enjoyed as much by the persecutor as the persecuted. Johnson enjoys a public fight, and Liverpudlians enjoy taking umbrage. Later, Johnson was forced to make an apology that became a media event.

But there was, even Liverpool enthusiasts concede, something valid in Johnson's criticisms. Liverpool is not the same as other cities – not even its near neighbours. The mentality of Liverpool is wholly different to that of Manchester yet the cities are only 30 miles apart, sharing similar climates and circumstances. Architecturally and socially, they developed very differently. The merchants who made Liverpool rich wanted to live near the city centre, close to the river and the ocean which define the place. Manchester's prosperous manufacturers pushed out to leafy suburbs and to rural Cheshire beyond. However, while Mancunians acquired a bluff, outgoing optimism, Liverpudlians have traditionally had an inclination to indulge in elective misery and voluntary self-deprecation, often of a most poetic kind.

Liverpool is more a city of architecture, art, poetry and humour than Manchester. Its architectural heritage is incomparable: less than a tenth the size of London, and with a much smaller fraction of its prosperity, Liverpool

has a disproportionately large number of listed buildings. The texture and grain of the place are real and you can feel them; they are not lazy tropes of architectural comment.

As for the state of the city – once proud, then ruined, now very probably resurgent – there is, indeed, much for artists, poets and humourists to use as inspirational material. The expressive range of Liverpool's built fabric goes from sublime to tragic, passing through melodramatic and absurd. It is unlike anywhere else, although it is much more like New York than, say, Paris. The music journalist Paul du Noyer is Liverpool's most astute critic and, with a contrariness typical of his native city, its most eloquent champion.

The religious dynamic of Liverpool is made into an architectural diagram by the spectacle of opposing Protestant and Catholic cathedrals at the poles of Hope Street, one of the city's great axes. The reddish-brown sandstone Gothic of the one stands in superlative contrast to the concrete Modernismo of the other, connected by Hope Street: Liverpool's bohemian artery. However, du Noyer says, 'inverted snobbery is the true religion of Liverpool'. For the city, urban depression is an art form; self-deprecation a style statement.

Is this cause or effect? Du Noyer says Liverpool's citizens have 'a peculiar streak of civic one-downmanship'. This is curious in a city in which, for the greater part of its history, exploration, wealth and power dominated the psychology. But even early historical reports on Liverpool often described pestilential

∧ The Roman Catholic and Anglican Cathedrals
PAUL MCMULLIN

∨ Ropewalks wayfinding
JOHN STONARD

lanes and vigorous cultures of vice and crime. In his *Condition of the Working Class in England* (1845), Marx's collaborator, Friedrich Engels, wrote of Liverpool's 'barbarity', and found 'the whole ordinarily very dirty and inhabited exclusively by proletarians'.

Bad conditions still exist, but misery is more stimulating to art than felicity. Liverpool's artists, du Noyer says, all want to 'turn rage into beauty'. So we return to Paul Birtill's poem, called 'A Memory of Liverpool':

His name was Jerry – horrible little man,
Got cancer of the throat at forty-four
And survived – one of the very small group
I believe
He used to say the best
Way of injuring someone in a pub
was to wait until they
put a glass to their
face and give it a hard shove.

That's very Liverpool, that 'hard shove'. By way of contrast, in his fine book, *Neo-Classicism* (1940), the supremely elegant essayist and literary critic Mario Praz compared Liverpool to Pompeii – a more elegant conceit. Praz, who became a majestic historian of style and interior design, once taught at the University of Liverpool. Was this Pompeian conceit a reference to the memory of lost magnificence, of a tragically interrupted destiny? After all, Pompeii had no future.

Does Liverpool? More so than any other place I know, Liverpool's future is connected to its past.

19

1
LIVERPOOL
PAST

Liverpool is for me an autobiography with buildings.

Growing up there was a real sentimental education.
The city taught me to think. And it taught me to think by
making me look. Liverpool has an almost overwhelming
physical character, not all of it good. Brooding, slovenly,
magnificent, romantic, miserable, tatty, funny, proud, heroic,
shameless, tragic and exciting in turns, it's a city that
demands a response. And mine was to become interested
in architecture and design.

I don't know any other city on earth with a greater variety of architecture. And beyond the variety, there is the architecture's distinctive power. 'Every Liverpudlian', Paul du Noyer says, 'carries a conviction of the city's extremity'. Quite so. For me, the extremes are ones of beauty and ugliness, great refinement and dismaying coarseness – but are rarely boring.

Liverpool is a city of architecture in several different senses. It is amazing, really, that it is to two Liverpool gentlemen that we owe, for example, our concepts of the Renaissance and Gothic.

It was William Roscoe, whose 1796 biography of Lorenzo de' Medici helped define the former, and architect Thomas Rickman who categorised the latter into the unforgettable Norman, Early English, Decorated and Perpendicular. Roscoe was, additionally, an outspokenly brave anti-slavery campaigner – this in a city, much of whose wealth was founded on the sinful profit margins made on the 'Middle Passage', the infernal stage of the slave-trade route that Liverpool served.

Two pubs are named after Roscoe. In fact, his father had been a publican on Mount Pleasant. Indeed, it is charmingly Liverpudlian that someone born in a pub became an international authority on Renaissance art and an early human-rights activist. In 1893, a Roscoe Professorship of Art was created at the city's university – perhaps the first such post in the country. Two years later, Liverpool had the first university school of architecture in the country. Liverpool also made civic design a legitimate academic subject; graduates in the discipline include Patrick Abercrombie and William Holford. The university's landmark 1892 Victoria Building by Alfred Waterhouse, incidentally, gave the world the expression 'redbrick' to denote Britain's regional, non-Oxbridge centres of learning.

^ Dale Street, c1900
LCC

^ St George's Hall, c1895
BLUECOAT PRESS

^ St Michael-in-the-Hamlet, Aigburth
JOHN STONARD

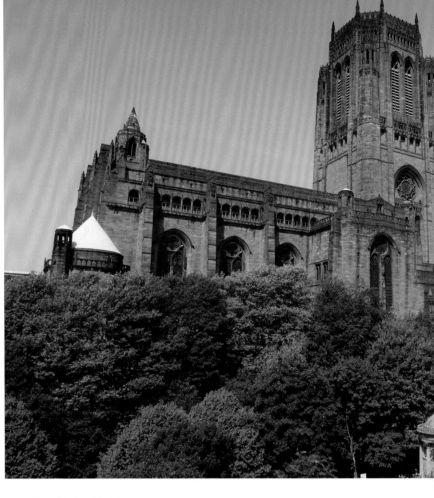

^ Liverpool Anglican Cathedral
PAUL MCMULLIN

Liverpool's architectural history is full of such facts and characters. However, Thomas Rickman is especially interesting. His St George's Church in St Domingo Road, Everton (1812–14) and his St Michael-in-the-Hamlet in Aigburth (1814–15) were both made of prefabricated components manufactured to his design by local ironmaster John Cragg, constituting an early form of 'system building'. Rickman's 1817 book, *An Attempt to Discriminate to the styles of architecture in England, from the Conquest to the Reformation*, established style labels that we still find useful. In Rickman, we find the combination of the entrepreneurial and the scholarly that is a Liverpool personality trait. Furthermore, between Rickman and Sir Giles Gilbert Scott's awesome Anglican

Cathedral you can find in Liverpool the entire history of the Gothic Revival.

What a curious hold Liverpool exerts. I rarely revisit, but it often 'revisits' me. I was born in Wales, have spent most of my life in London and merely went to school in Liverpool, but I still regard it as home. Certainly, memories of Liverpool are disproportionately large in my mental landscape, in my dreams. Long before I knew the word, Scott's cathedral taught me the scary idea of The Sublime from first principles.

I have no family in Liverpool and my friends remain only as ghosts, but I nonetheless often toy with the idea of going back. I left, restless, aged 17; it was only later that

∧ Interior of Martins Bank
PAUL MCMULLIN

∨ Martins Bank Building, Water Street under construction 1927-32
LCC

I realised that Liverpool's vast presence had made me interested in architecture. As a child, I realised before I even knew what design meant that one composition of bricks, stone and glass was magnificent and exciting – and that another could be soul-destroying.

Liverpool is a city of unusual scale. As Quentin Hughes – the Liverpool-Welsh architect-soldier-historian-conservationist, whose *Seaport* (1964) is one of the best city biographies in any language – explained, Liverpool's centre is 'wide and expansive', unlike anywhere else south of Edinburgh. Liverpool has been called the 'New York of Europe'. This reputation has an element of pathos: many Jews escaping Eastern European pogroms were swindled into believing that Liverpool was America, and forcibly disembarked 3,000 miles short of their longed-for destination. One of their descendants became famous as manager of The Beatles.

∧ The Greek Orthodox Church
PAUL MCMULLIN

The Jewish novelist Linda Grant described her grandparents' arrival in the city:

Even used to the baroque splendour of Warsaw … visited from the agrarian plains of the east, [my grandfather] was staggered by the city at which he had made landfall. New York! He cried. The greatest city on earth! The splendour of its architecture bearing down on this pogrom immigrant.

But there is a more positive aspect to Liverpool's geography and position: the city quite literally looks to America, not to Europe. The Atlantic Ocean is a significant presence, both commercially and culturally.

Of about five and a half million transatlantic emigrants in the second half of the 19th century, roughly four and three-quarter million went via Liverpool. There is a statue of Christopher Columbus outside the Palm House in Sefton Park. On its plinth is the inscription: 'The discoverer of America was the maker of Liverpool'. The economic reality of this was that, between 1699 and 1807, Liverpool traders exported 1,364,930 unwilling Africans on 5,249 voyages to slavery in the American colonies (later, the United States), enduring the fearful 'Middle Passage'.

During the Second World War, the Western Approaches Command Room, which managed the Battle of the Atlantic, was based in Derby House at Exchange Flags in the commercial district.

The very first British encounter of the war was the sinking of the SS *Athenia* en route from Liverpool to Canada. This came within 24 hours of the declaration of hostilities between Britain and Germany, on 3 September 1939. I realise now – significantly – that one of my father's favourite books was Nicholas Monsarrat's *The Cruel Sea* (1951), the naval classic which describes the Atlantic convoys that set out from the Mersey. Monsarrat was born in Liverpool in 1910.

The architecture of my dreams (and nightmares) is that of Liverpool. Epic, melancholy, social and economic tumult and stunning physical presence do not necessarily make a happy city, but they do make a memorable one. Each of Liverpool's characteristics is revealed in one or other of its monuments. Neuro-aestheticians know that architecture and memory are closely related: building plans seem somehow to correlate with structures in the brain. Furthermore, architectural elevations are, surely, the most evocative visual art form. John Lennon knew this too. His 'In My Life' is one of the great songs about place. Some may rate Gershwin's 'Manhattan' more sophisticated, but Lennon's Liverpool is surely more moving.

'In My Life' was recorded October 1965, and was inspired by the television presenter Kenneth Alsop telling Lennon that he should spend more time focusing on his interior life. The song describes a journey that began at Lennon's childhood home in Menlove Avenue (a smart semi called 'Mendip's' recently acquired by The

< Aquitania at the landing stage, c1920
LCC

26

National Trust, not the hardscrabble cold-water walk-up of our imaginations). His destination was the 'Dockers' Umbrella', the local name for the old Overhead Railway – 17 stations over seven miles: 'the first and fastest electric railway in the world' – that was demolished in 1958. The life of the Overhead, modelled on New York's 'El' almost exactly matched Liverpool's great years. (In 1896, Lumière used it for one of cinema's first tracking shots.)

For Lennon, it was an immensely significant song – the first one he took really seriously. First drafts of the journey included an architectural gazetteer listing: Penny Lane, Church Road, the clock tower, Abbey Cinema, tram sheds, Dutch café, St Columba's Church and Calderstone's Park. In the writing, Lennon became moved by the idea that the familiar landscapes of his childhood were fast disappearing. In the next draft of the song, the named landmarks or monuments were excluded. In their place was a beautiful song about loss and mourning, death, decay, memory and the ineffable monument. Lennon's words are :

There are places I'll remember
All my life though some have changed

Some forever not for better
Some have gone and some remain
All these places have their moments
With lovers and friends I still can recall
Some are dead and some are living
In my life I've loved them all.

This, according to Beatles critic Steve Turner, may have been inspired by Charles Lamb's 'The Old Familiar Faces', which every schoolboy used to know from Palgrave's *Golden Treasury*. Lennon would certainly have seen a copy in the Quarry Bank School library. (Quarry Bank was the eccentric school, modelled on Eton, where Lennon framed his rebellion against a backdrop of mortarboards and Latin Prep.) Lamb's poem includes the lines:

I have had playmates, I have had companions
In my days of childhood, in my joyful
school-days;
All, all are gone, the old familiar faces . . . .
How some they have died and some they have left me,
And some are taken from me; all are departed; All, all
are gone, the old familiar faces.

ˇ Overhead Railway in 1951
BLUECOAT PRESS

∧ Old Haymarket, 1928 and the view towards the River Mersey
BLUECOAT PRESS

The Beatles have, it seems, as many historical layers as their native Liverpool.

Lennon's memories and mine were based on real experience, but, curiously, Liverpool seems to have some sort of occult power even to influence people who never knew the city. Literature has several examples of imaginative accounts of real places: Edgar Allan Poe's 'The Coliseum' and Franz Kafka's *Amerika* are obvious examples. In 1824, Gaetano Donizetti wrote an opera called *Emilia di Liverpool,* but no one seems certain exactly why – or whether the great composer actually visited Merseyside. However, no urban fantasy is surely so curious as Carl Gustav Jung's Liverpool. Jung may have visited Liverpool in 1927; it's not absolutely clear. But what is certain is that he imagined the city. In *Memories, Dreams and Reflections,* he wrote:

I found myself in a dark, sooty city. It was night, and winter, and dark and raining. I was in Liverpool. With a number of Swiss – say half a dozen – I walked through the dark streets. I had the feeling that we were coming from the harbour and that the real city was actually above, on the cliffs. We climbed up there. It reminded me of Basel, where the market is down below and you go up through the Totengässchen [Alley of the Dead] which leads to a plateau above and so to the Petersplatz and the Peterskirche. When we reached the plateau,

we found a broad square dimly illuminated by the street lights into which many streets converged. The various quarters of the city were arranged radially around that square.

It was from here (and he seems to have been talking about the area around Mathew Street, later well known as the site of the famous Cavern Club) that Jung saw an island with a single magnolia tree. He explained:

This dream represented my situation at the time. I can still see the greyish-yellow raincoats, glistening in the wetness of the rain. Everything was extremely unpleasant, black and opaque – just as I felt then. But I had a vision of unearthly beauty and that was why I was able to live at all. Liverpool is the pool of life.

When did Liverpool begin to develop its distinctive character? The first famous description of the city appears in Daniel Defoe's *A Tour through the Whole Island of Great Britain* in 1724–6. Defoe wrote:

The inhabitants have of late years, and since the visible increase of their trade, made a large basin or wet dock, at the east end of the town, where, at an immense charge, the place considered, they have brought the tide from the Mersee to flow up by an opening that looks to the south and the ships go in to the north; so that the town entirely shelters it from the westerly and northerly

28

^ Dock Wall detail
PAUL MCMULLIN

^ Exterior of Albert
Dock, c1978
ANTHONY PRICE/LCC

winds, the hills from the easterly, and the ships lye, as in a mill-pond, with the utmost safety and convenience.

Defoe is writing of Liverpool Corporation's 1715 'Old Dock'. While London, Plymouth and Portsmouth already had naval wet docks, Liverpool's was the first dedicated to trade. In this way was the character of the city established. The Atlantic Ocean and the docks that serviced it define Liverpool. In the early 19th century, the necessity of protecting valuable goods from accidental conflagration led to pioneering fireproof construction methods in warehouses. In 1824, Jesse Hartley, architect of the Albert Dock, became the world's first civilian dock engineer. When Albert Dock was opened on 30 July 1846, Prince Albert said, 'I have heard of

the greatness of Liverpool, but the reality far surpasses the experience'. The city also boasted the world's first hydraulic cargo-handling systems. Largely as a result of Liverpool's commitment to maritime commerce, by the middle of the 19th century Britain was responsible for about 25 per cent of world trade.

But what of the unique Liverpool character – linguistic and architectural? Although Heathcliff, Emily Brontë's turbulent hero in *Wuthering Heights*, her 1847 blockbuster, was a Liverpudlian (or at least, a foundling saved from Liverpool's streets by the Earnshaw family), it is unlikely he had a Liverpool accent. Linguistics experts believe that it was only after the mid-19th century that the local accent – under the influence of Irish, Welsh

< Albert Dock
hydraulic hoist,
c1978
PAUL MCMULLIN

29

and Chinese immigration – began to separate itself from generic Lancashire. From here, it was a small step to the glorious vernacular surrealism that informs the local language. 'A Hard Day's Night' was not poetic invention; nor was 'yellow matter custard'. That's just, Paul du Noyer notes, the way they speak.

Two centuries ago, the city's architectural character was already taking shape. Liverpool has a fine Palladian town hall by John Wood the Younger of Bath (1749, reconstructed 1807), which seems almost incongruously delicate in its tough and massive surroundings. Then there is the superb St George's Hall by the tragic young genius Harvey Lonsdale Elmes. This vast temple of urban pride, the result of an ambitious 1839 competition, is routinely and correctly described as Europe's greatest Neo-Classical building, but its history was marked by the sort of politicking that has ever since troubled architects in Liverpool. The unknown and untried Elmes, a Londoner, won the ambitious civic competition when he was 21 with a design of total artistic authority.

Nonetheless, Liverpool's stage army of interfering politicos scandalously refused to believe that the

sickly, young architect could supervise the demanding works, and, after humiliating interferences, Elmes died romantically. Liverpool handed the project to the sedate and experienced Charles Robert Cockerell, later designer of Liverpool's branch of The Bank of England. The St George's Hall episode has become a case study in the vagaries of the architect's status and responsibilities. It has also been sardonically remarked that only in Liverpool would you find the major public building devoted explicitly to music and crime (as St George's Hall accommodates both a vast Minton-tiled concert hall and the city's criminal courts).

However, while St George's Hall is a powerful expression of preening urban vanity, the wonder of Liverpool is the business district and the waterfront, now a World Heritage Site. Here, the first great set piece was the Albert Dock, one of the great monuments of the functionalist tradition in English vernacular architecture. It was designed and built between 1844 and 1847 by Jesse Hartley. Architectural historian Nikolaus Pevsner said: 'For sheer punch there is little in the early commercial architecture of Europe to emulate it'.

31

We admire it for its structural clarity, monumental presence and technical ingenuity. Because it was designed to hold valuable goods from the Far East trade, it was made of non-combustible materials using techniques borrowed from cotton mills. Hartley put a brick skin around an iron frame on top of 5,300 beech piles. The roof is a stressed-iron structure of ingenious design. The vaguely Doric, fluteless columns, which add so much to a sense of muscularity, are hollow cast iron.

Albert Dock became a symbol of Liverpool's romantic decline when Quentin Hughes published evocative, grainy photographs of its derelict state in *Seaport*. These taught a generation (myself included) what beauty there might be in neglect, and what fine architecture might be produced on functional principles. Albert Dock is admired by us today for its handsome, no-nonsense strength and its symbolic force, but Liverpool's resident petulant Victorian intellectual, an architectural historian called Joseph Picton, regarded it as a 'simply hideous pile of naked brickwork'. Liverpool has something of a tradition in treating the great architects who work there with contempt.

In fact, Albert Dock's real life was short. By the late 19th century, its fixed structure was too small for the new generation of ships and by the time of the First World War no ships were unloading there. By the 1960s, when Quentin Hughes's photographer went to work, demolition was in prospect. On this site in 1966, the notorious developer Harry Hyams and his architect Richard Seifert proposed 'River City', which included a 42-storey tower.

Although the Hyams-and-Seifert combination is ritually repudiated, their proposals for the moribund Liverpool docks were visionary and might have retarded the city's decline, if not necessarily accelerating its prospects. Unsurprisingly, 'River City' was immediately mired in controversy and obfuscation. The Albert Dock finally closed in 1972, but, undaunted by flim-flam, in the late 1970s Seifert was back, proposing the world's tallest building at 560 metres (1,831 feet) in height. Again, this would have been a real benefit for Liverpool, in terms of symbolism if nothing else, but an alternative direction was taken for the city's regeneration.

Instead of giddying high-rise, in 1983 it was decided to do 'creative reuse' on Albert Dock. Instead of up,

ˇ The Albert Dock
PAUL MCMULLIN

∧ Custom House as seen from Salthouse Dock, c1895
BLUECOAT PRESS

∨ The Seifert proposal for the Albert Dock site, c1966
LCC

Liverpool went back. In the early 1980s, The Tate Gallery was working on expansionist plans to turn itself into a national art franchise. James Stirling, a Liverpudlian and graduate of the city's school of architecture who was also a student of Quarry Bank (Lennon's old school), was working on London's new Clore Gallery at the original Tate (now Tate Britain) on London's Millbank, and won the commission to adapt Jesse Hartley's fine old fireproof warehouses into a modern art gallery. Stirling reticently respected Hartley's monument: the intrinsic honesty, explicit muscularity and emphatic red-brick and industrial finishes of the original nicely complemented his own powerful architectural aesthetic. In vivid blue and orange with bold typography, Tate Liverpool comprises that rarest of things: the reuse of an old building which is both sympathetic and indisputably modern as well. It was completed in 1988.

Albert Dock is next door to the Pier Head site that once housed the old George's Dock. In a similar manner to Albert Dock, but roughly 100 years earlier, this had become obsolete by the late 19th century – and so an opportunity arose to redevelop. The result on that occasion was a waterfront assemblage of buildings to rival those of New York or Venice. Pevsner talks of Durban and Hong Kong, but for once he is understating. How did this trio of monuments – now known a might too cutely as 'The Three Graces' – come about?

When drained and filled, the old George's Dock offered a wonderful riverside site, whose irregular plan encouraged a variety of architectural approaches. The Edwardian 'moment' combined Victorian wealth and conviction with a more modern commercial awareness. It was the purpose of all its very competitive clients

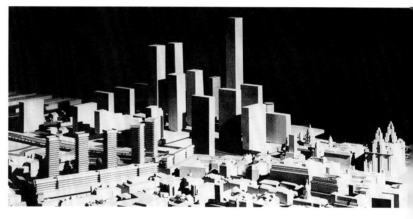

∨ Exterior of Tate Gallery, Albert Dock
JOHN STONARD

∧∧ Details on Cunard Building
PAUL MCMULLIN

∧ The Pier Head in 1960
BLUECOAT PRESS

and their architects to make monuments, to create landmarks for the comings and goings that define the melancholy and magnificence of Liverpool and its sometimes mawkishly sentimental mentality. However, it was also their purpose to advertise their businesses. The Pier Head buildings embody what today we would call 'corporate identity', or architecture as an element of branding – both of themselves and of the city as a whole.

First to build was the Mersey Docks and Harbour Board. Founded in 1857, this was the first non-profit dock-management organisation in the world. It required a headquarters of appropriate pomp and by 1907, when work began, the rhetoric of Edwardian Baroque was well able to achieve a suitable level of pomposity. Its architects were Arnold Thornley working with Briggs and Wolstenholme. Their design comprised a steel frame encased in Portland stone, with portentous domes taken directly from C. H. Reilly's design for the Anglican Cathedral competition of 1902.

Next came the famous Liver Building, which was designed very deliberately to upstage the Mersey Docks and Harbour Board building. Its architect was Walter Aubrey Thomas, who had previously worked

on the 1906 State Fire Assurance Offices in nearby Dale Street. The Liver Building employed an advanced ferro-concrete frame by the engineers Mouchel, using technology established by reinforced-concrete pioneer François Hennebique. It was cast on site, and one floor of Britain's first skyscraper (actually thus called) was realised every 19 days. It is a building of absolute originality and unforgettable presence.

Lastly, on the site that was acquired by the Cunard Steamship Company in 1914: a 'third Grace'. Like the Liver Building, the Cunard Office's construction is ferro-concrete with deeply incised Portland stone cladding: an 'Italian palazzo draped in Greek Revival detail', according to Quentin Hughes. Authorship is confused, but its designers were probably Mewes and Davis with a nod across the Atlantic to Neo-Classicists McKim Mead and White. (So much of Liverpool's business district looks like a metropolis of the American Midwest, rather than of Europe.)

World Heritage sites seldom, however, arise with no trace of controversy. The original Cunard competition design was abandoned, and the Mersey Docks and Harbour Board contest was announced only after the sort of aggressive debate which predicted the recent hoo-ha

over the new Museum of Liverpool. Robert Gladstone, grandee of the Docks, feared his corporate prestige was threatened by the encroaching Liver Building. He sniffily wrote: 'Unless a very considerable reduction is made in the height of the building, the fine architectural effect of the Dock Offices would be completely spoiled and the whole waterfront architectural effect would be squandered'. He was wrong. Then, the *Architectural Review* criticised the entire Pier Head for its lack of harmony and balance – not to mention its contrasting styles, materials and scales. Professor Charles Reilly said the Pier Head was 'one of the best, or worst, examples of excessive individualism in architecture'. So, Liverpool's lesson to world architecture is that lack of balance and harmony, contrasting styles and materials plus excessive individualism seem to be the specification for masterpieces of cityscape.

The three make superb compositions and fine contrasts. However, almost as soon as they were finished Liverpool began its long period of decline. What wasn't caused by the sort of historical forces Marx would have understood was brought about by the Luftwaffe. There exists some evidence that Adolf Hitler may have lived in Liverpool (at 102 Upper Stanhope Street in Toxteth) in 1912–13. Indisputably, his half-brother Alois lived in Liverpool with his Irish wife, Bridget, and their son, William Patrick Hitler. Some say that because of a memory of unhappiness on Merseyside, Hitler's *Terrorflieger* were ordered to unleash an unusually ferocious version of the *Blitzkrieg* on Liverpool.

The Blitz against Liverpool began on 1 May 1941. Never mind the dreadful physical destruction, it was psychological warfare too – designed to demoralise. In the course of a single week, 681 Heinkels, Junkers and Dorniers dropped 870 tonnes of high explosives as well as 112,000 incendiary bombs onto the city of Scousers. With 15,000 blitzed sites, Liverpool had more bomb damage than any British city other than London.

One of these sites was St Luke's on Leece Street, a handsome Neo-Gothic church designed by local architect, Grand Tourist and socialite John Foster, who was also the architect of a pretty little Greek temple above the canyon surrounding the Anglican Cathedral. (Karl Friedrich Schinkel visited Foster in 1826.) Construction of St Luke's began on 9 April 1811; on 5 May 1941, it was completely gutted. St Luke's has remained a haunting memorial shell ever since, not unlike the Kaiser-Wilhelm-Gedächtnis-Kirche off Berlin's Kurfürstendamm. The Blitz destruction left Liverpool with only memories of its magnificence. I grew up there at a time when bomb damage was still obvious everywhere.

∧∧ The Pier Head buildings with the recently completed canal link
PAUL MCMULLIN

∧ The Victoria Monument and South Castle Street in 1945
BLUECOAT PRESS

Tragically, until very recently the sheer monumentality of the city's surviving monuments and the desolation of war humbled and hobbled the imaginations of those yearning to restore lost glories. However, in reality the creative malaise probably started even earlier. When I was a student, we all used to say how shaming it was that we could think of no new monuments in the city since the end of the First World War. In fact, although the Liverpool University School of Architecture welcomed Eric(h) Mendelsohn and Walter Gropius as refugees from Hitler's Germany, the Modern Movement had little influence on the city. The great inter-war social-housing projects by Lancelot Keay might have been reminiscent of Karl Ehn's Karl Marx Hof in Vienna, but Liverpool has no International Style buildings from the period between the wars. Still, it is pleasing to reflect on a conservative council eccentrically aping Ehn's continental building, whose political character was so unambiguous that it was known as 'The Red Fortress'. Again, only in Liverpool.

What Liverpool does have in place of the International Style is Herbert Rowse's India Buildings, his ineffable Mersey Tunnel and his Philharmonic Hall in the Amsterdam Style of Dudok. Indeed, on the evidence of these three edifices alone Herbert J. Rowse may be one of the most neglected great architects of the mid-20th century. And then there is Speke Airport (1933) by R. Arthur Landstein of the City Surveyor's office, modelled, like Keay's social housing, on Ehn's continental example. Speke, like all Liverpool's great buildings, is utterly distinctive. But the most distinctive of all is surely the Mersey Tunnel, one of the strangest 'buildings' in the

^ The entrance to the Mersey Tunnel, 1935
BLUECOAT PRESS

world, opened on 18 July 1934. At 3.4 kilometres (2.13 miles), it was at the time the longest underwater tunnel in the world. I remember now with a mixture of fascination and terror its cream ceramic tiles, its distinctive smell and its strange Art Deco detailing.

And still I have left so much out of this short account of this city of dreams and nightmares, the half-remembered place that made me interested in architecture. There is the supremely elegant, Georgian Rodney Street, almost a mirror image of Dublin, where future Prime Minister William Ewart Gladstone was born at No. 62. On the nightmare side, there is the horrible canyon that is St James' Cemetery (1825–9) by John Foster, where the catacombs suggest a Roman scale and ambition. Adapted from a disused quarry, terrifying Piranesian ramps are provided for funeral processions. Here, Foster designed a memorial to Liverpool MP William Huskisson, the first railway fatality – killed by

the Rocket on its initial outing for the Liverpool and Manchester Railway on 15 September 1830. Although this proto-modern event established four feet eight and a half inches (nowadays, 1.4 metres) as the near-universal railway gauge, Huskisson is depicted anachronistically in a Roman toga.

However, Henry Booth, one of the promoters of the railway, sensed the future: 'what was quick is now slow; what was distant is now near'. That was 19th-century Liverpool's view of the world. This cemetery gave me a terrible sense of The Sublime, just as John Foster's delightful mortuary chapel within it, a perfect Greek miniature, gave a sense of the exotic. Sublimity and terror were augmented with the sheer 20th-century thrill caused by the appearance of Giles Gilbert Scott's forbiddingly vast Anglican Cathedral above the overgrown, infernal canyon. Even today, it seems an improbable building. It is delightfully odd that the

< Rodney Street
PAUL McMULLIN

37

same man who designed this, one of the largest Gothic structures in the world, also designed one of the most popular and compact Classicist ones: the old Post Office telephone box, a miniature in the style of Sir John Soane. Scott was for a while a lecturer in the Liverpool School of Architecture, and he used the cathedral site visits to teach students: each detail, he explained, was drawn 1:1 by himself so that craftsmen could make zinc templates of the assemblages.

It was also in Liverpool that I discovered Nikolaus Pevsner one Saturday in 1966, when Pelican published the latest edition of *Pioneers of Modern Design*. I bought it in the book department of Lewis's Department Store and started reading that afternoon while standing underneath Epstein's hilarious *Spirit of Liverpool Resurgent*, the statue of an emphatically naked youth standing on a prow of a ship that stands above the entrance to the store (which had been flattened by a landmine in 1941).

It was Pevsner who taught me about Peter Ellis, Liverpool's unlikely prototype Modernist. Here, in Oriel Chambers on Water Street in 1864, he built an astonishing, unprecedentedly early design of cantilevered cladding. The apparently modular windows project out 750 mm (two foot six inches) from the frame. Inside, lay what Charles Reilly called 'cellular habitation'; outside, a frank prediction of skyscraper style with bold, plate-glass windows reflecting the surrounding buildings.

Later, I learnt about other Liverpudlian firsts in building technology. There was David Boswell Reid's air-management system in St George's Hall, derived from expertise acquired in ventilating the hulls of transatlantic ships. When it was opened in 1851, Lime Street Railway Station was the world's widest iron-spanned structure. The Royal Insurance Building, begun in 1897, was one of the first and largest steel-framed buildings in Britain, and Martin's Bank had a fine early example of low-temperature ceiling heating.

^ Peter Ellis Building, 16 Cook Street
PAUL MCMULLIN

^ The glass enclosed staircase at the rear of 16 Cook Street
PAUL MCMULLIN

And I learnt about Modernism too. Most of all, however, it was not Pevsner's Modernism but that of a local architect, Gerald R. Beech, that excited me. In 1960, on Beaconsfield Road (the site of the Strawberry Fields that interested John Lennon) Beech and Dewi Prys Thomas built a small Modernist house that became the *Woman's Journal* House of the Year in 1960. It was exquisite: there were plants and reflecting pools. There was 'Scandiwegian' furniture, a ground floor with brickwork in a white 'Tyrolean' finish and timber-clad, jettied-out upper parts. It became a place of pilgrimage for me. So too was the Whitley Lang and Neil machine tool factory in Speke, a glass-walled pavilion which put the machinery on philosophically modern display 20 years and more before Nicholas Grimshaw had the same idea with *The Financial Times* printworks in east London.

Best of all was the Wyncote Sports Pavilion of 1961–2 on Mather Avenue. Here, the university invested in clarity, lightness and optimism: a boxy, cantilevered pavilion – glazed, oversailing, a little Japanese. Then there was the University Department of Electrical Engineering and Electronics (1963–6) with signature white tiles and

bronze windows by YRM. There was Denys Lasdun's University Sports Centre of 1966. A short walk in the city centre could give those willing to learn a unique lesson in modern architectural history an example of almost everything. I remember now how very proud this made me feel of Liverpool's commitment to modernity. So – universities could be enlightened patrons!

But so too could local authorities. I haunted Allerton Branch Library, built by Ronald Bradbury, City Architect in 1964–5, in a style that cannot now be described but that seemed to me at the time to be the last word in architectural enlightenment. There, beneath the blue suburban skies I complemented Quarry Bank's Classical education by reading glossy books about advertising in an environment that I remember as perpetual sunshine and light wood. In 1969, as I was leaving Liverpool, James L. Roberts's St John's Beacon, a chimney disguised as a revolving restaurant, emerged from the old St John's Market. It seemed tawdry at the time. Ten years later, Liverpool reached the bottom. In Paul du Noyer's words, it seemed that 'the city itself had lost its job'.

Until now, that is. Liverpool is building again.

v Liverpool One construction with St John's Beacon, 2007
PAUL MCMULLIN

2
LIVERPOOL
PRESENT

For someone brought up at a time when 'Liverpool' was a synonym for urban misery, the new state of the city astonishes. There is a vitality and confidence perhaps not felt since the days of the ocean liners and sugar barons. The change of mood is welcome and exhilarating, but also unsettling. For 50 years, Liverpool was a notably unsuccessful laboratory for almost every school of urban planning.

< View down Wall Street from Paradise Street
PAUL MCMULLIN

^ Shennan Plan of c1945
LCC

^ Shankland plan of 1965
LCC

The old Liverpool had the very best and the very worst of what a city can possess: a huge weight of architectural history scarcely balanced by contemporary equivalents. That balance is now changing, but some fainthearts fear Liverpool may be turning itself into a graveyard for inappropriate architectural experiment.

Others ask if this is a new Liverpool – or an evolution of the old one. Of course, all cities – except Venice – evolve, but Liverpool's case is exceptional, as its citizens insist. Few cities anywhere have experienced such contrasts of wealth and poverty, of felicity and misery. Accordingly, the current regeneration of Liverpool prompts exceptional questions about an exceptional city. Does architecture make the city or does the city make its architecture? How many of the recent landmark buildings truly stand comparison with the city's famous monuments?

After the calamities of the Blitz, Liverpool's Alfred Shennan (a rare combination of councillor and architect, now known for his Art Deco cinemas) addressed The Civic Society about how the city might be rebuilt. In a euphoria of Britain-Can-Make-It futurism, he spoke of four-lane inner ring roads connecting the city centre's

landmarks; there would be vast, European boulevards in the style of Barcelona, Paris and Vienna. Cars would travel this urban motorway at 50 miles an hour! There would be multi-storey car parks for 36,000 vehicles. There would be shopping precincts! Shennan's plan was abandoned early on in favour of piecemeal development within the city centre, as sparse funds were diverted to housing and industrialisation.

However, in 1965 it was replaced by the even more radical City Centre Plan of Graeme Shankland. People in Triumph Heralds and Ford Cortinas would cruise inner ring roads and park happily. It seems incredible now, but such was the appetite for renewal that even the conservation-minded architect Quentin Hughes looked forward to it. Shankland's vision was to be made writ by Walter Bor, City Planning Officer, 1964–7, but – this being Liverpool – the plan was never properly realised because the city's money was diverted into the docks, but with less vision and to poorer effect than that which accompanied the dock investment of the past.

When Rotterdam's Europoort suddenly became a more convenient base for the new containerised trade, Liverpool's docks were doomed. A city that had always looked to North America got one of its many come-uppances as the European Union (EU) became a trading reality. As early as 1952, the architectural critic Colin Boyne was scathing about Liverpool as a business prospect. It had nothing to attract developers, he said. And after Rotterdam, it had not a lot to attract merchants. The city's half-built urban freeways were never connected to the North's 'central nervous system', the M62 motorway. This left Liverpool both symbolically and practically stranded just as it entered its period of maximum economic wretchedness. And the large-scale clearances were left as gaping wounds in the city's anatomy, becoming monuments not to civic pride and ambition but rather to the horrors of planning blight.

In addition, there was the wrongheadedness of 'overspill'. While housing in its own city centre was abject and begging for attention, Liverpool got itself three new satellite towns in Winsford, Skelmersdale and Runcorn. Architectural writer Brian Hatton described this depopulating overspill policy as the equivalent of curing anaemia by bleeding.

A heroic civic redesign by Colin St John Wilson was commissioned, then opportunistically abandoned in 1961 when investors offered to redevelop – although some would say 'destroy' – the old St John's Market where once I met George the Hammer Man at a bar. On account of its urban misery, Liverpool – the city of Renaissance Studies, Gothic taxonomy, Atlantic trade, Britain's first skyscraper and The Beatles – was humiliatingly given Objective One Status by the European Union. A city gets the dubious status of Objective One if it suffers from low investment, weak infrastructure, high unemployment and bad services. Liverpool did.

Simon Allford of architectural practice Allford Hall Monaghan Morris (AHMM) described his Liverpool thus:

As its once vital economy crumbled, Liverpool suffered more noisily than the other great Northern cities. The magnificent grid-iron core of bustling commercial and civic monuments, the docks and the set-piece urban wrap of housing, parks and cathedrals were, even by the swinging sixties, becoming denuded of life. The life that survives was often confined to the cramped Victorian terraces and a sense of hopelessness and bitterness was encouraged by the flight to dreary overspill. Liverpool became the symbol of a national problem.

ˇ Upper Parliament Street Clearance, 1977
LCC

∧ Mann island
PAUL MCMULLIN

∧ The Pier Head from the new Liverpool Museum steps
PAUL MCMULLIN

It is in this context that the regeneration of Liverpool needs to be understood. 'If you want things to stay the same, they are going to have to change' is the best line in Giuseppe di Lampedusa's *The Leopard*, his posthumous masterpiece about *Risorgimento-era* Sicily, in which architecture is used to evoke mood. Ruin was an inspiration to Lampedusa. It eventually became an inspiration in Liverpool. Liverpool proves that old trope: we fashion our cities and then they fashion us. The old Liverpool inspired Jung, Hitler and Lennon – and, if it does not read immodestly in such company, me. We have all enjoyed, and will continue to enjoy, Liverpool's incomparable history and the buildings that are its record, but we have to believe that we can make new monuments, not just meditate on the old ones. Happily, this is now happening. The result is not perfect, but it is inspiring.

The current regeneration began on 5 June 1999, when the City Council advertised in *The Estates Gazette and The Financial Times*, inviting expressions of interest in the desolate and shabby 'Bluecoat Triangle'. Four years later, on 3 June 2003, there was an additional fillip when it was announced that Liverpool would be European Capital of Culture in 2008. Although not directly productive of any new buildings, this very visible deadline provided an imperative. Furthermore, 2008 generated some impressive statistics, even if the Capital of Culture programme began as a 'Scouse wedding' in the words of its director, Phil Redmond – a Scouse wedding being an event in which, traditionally, a lot of people get together, drink an immoderate amount, argue, fight, hit each other and then make it up with gushing sentiment.

The economic impact of the Capital of Culture year was nearly a positive billion. Tate Liverpool in Albert Dock, for 20 years the anchor of regeneration, attracted more than one million visitors, the majority of them for the

first time. Seventy-nine per cent of correspondents investigated in one poll thought Liverpool was on the way up, while *Condé Nast Traveller,* a magazine more used to carrying articles about yacht charter in the Bahamas and spas in Puglia, stated that Liverpool was third only to London and Edinburgh as a British urban attraction.

However, the architectural story of Liverpool's regeneration has been sometimes hesitant – and, typical of the city, often prosecuted in a mood of contrariness and contumely. The muddled story of what became known as 'The Fourth Grace' illustrated the new Liverpool in all its international glory and provincial confusion. Since the guarded optimism suggested by the terms of the 1947 Town and Country Planning Act – drafted by Liverpool alumni Abercrombie and Holford – there has been continual discussion about how Liverpool can augment its magnificent waterfront.

By 2002, a site became available where once stood a Mercedes-Benz showroom and the car park of the Merseyside Maritime Museum. It was, the officials said, 'one of the world's most inspiring development opportunities'. And everyone recognised that the 'challenge [was] to provide an iconic world-class building or buildings of the twenty-first century' in order to match the existing Pier Head ensemble.

In 2003, the urban-regeneration company Liverpool Vision called the project 'The Fourth Grace', an allusion to classical mythology: The Three Graces were the sisters Aglaia, Thalia and Euphrosyne, who were the embodiment of beauty and charm and whose duty was to redistribute these happy characteristics. Shortlisted entries to the competition came from Richard Rogers, Foster and Partners, Edward Cullinan and Will Alsop. Against the confident Modernism of the first three, Alsop's imaginative and unusual solution looked eccentric. He did not seek to dominate the skyline, but hid 340 flats, a hotel, retail and leisure – plus a sculpture park about the history of Liverpool – in six 'zones'. It was a far less developed idea than those of the other architects: deliberately allusive, sculptural and experimental (Alsop begins his designs as paintings), it was called 'The Cloud'. In fact, it was a concept more than a finished design – so much so that in public consultation, it was placed last by citizen-critics who perhaps could not construe the architect's imaginative intentions. Yet, to a mixture of surprise, delight and consternation, 'The Cloud' won.

There were reservations from the start, and the architect had soon to promise redesigns. Alas, the project unfolded like that famous Scouse wedding: argument and calamity were guests at the ceremony and in 2004 the project was abandoned, the officials citing out-of-control costs in an overambitious, but ill-formed, design. Alsop was naturally outraged. He described his reaction:

Liverpool… oh Liverpool. A beguiling city of former courage and pride. A place that at one time firmly believed it could challenge London as a centre of wealth, culture and power. A self-belief that allowed it to develop a fabric of difficult and challenging buildings which leaves it today as a wonderful museum of the past. A mausoleum that contains people who are a shadow of their forefathers. A city that argues with itself and consistently shoots itself in the foot. The Liverpudlians do not deserve such a wonderful place. My Fourth Grace building was unceremoniously dumped by the council because of lack of public support. NOT TRUE. They could not afford their share of the cost because they had overspent on King's Dock. They blame the architect and not themselves, something that the former generation would never have done. Sadly I still love the city. I love the past in this place. I do not love their regeneration projects now. They lack bravado and quality. Previously Liverpool possessed both.

On a site near where Alsop's Cloud sadly evaporated, Wilkinson Eyre's Liverpool Arena has become the boldest new building in the city and a significant extension of the glorious waterfront's iconography. It is an open clamshell, with complex double curvatures which some people see as a graphic of a swimmer. The two half shells are connected by an atrium; a glazed base reflects the concourse, and bands of metal and glass dominate its surface effect. The airy, cross-vaulted steel skeleton supporting the roof offers a contrasting architectural language. Seen from the Mersey, it is 'bookended' by the two cathedrals in the distance, and its near neighbour is the Albert Dock. It is a characterful addition to what's known as The King's Waterfront. A mixture of auditoriums and conference centre, unlike European rivals in Milan and London's Excel, Liverpool's Arena is in the symbolic heart of the city. But the Arena's architects have mixed feelings about their experience in the city.

Chris Wilkinson told me that the Alsop Affair 'left some nervousness' among architects wanting to work in Liverpool. Wilkinson has known Liverpool since he used to do crits at the school of architecture in Abercromby Square. The city made a strong impression, as it so often does. 'An exciting place to visit', Wilkinson told me, '… but a bit bleak'.

Wilkinson Eyre is a firm of architects with a justified reputation for technical meticulousness, entirely different in character to Alsop's formal bravura. They like titanium lock-nuts and tensioned guy wires, not colourful

ᵛ Aerial view of the Liverpool Arena and Convention Centre
PAUL MCMULLIN

ᵛ Riverside entrance of the Arena and Convention Centre
PAUL MCMULLIN

broad-brush treatments. The practice's aspirations were high and explicit, but Chris Wilkinson found the local press very tough, consistently and cheerfully predicting disaster for his technically ambitious design. Acutely aware of the traditions and of the privileges and constraints of working on a World Heritage Site, Wilkinson commented:

The Albert Dock? What a great place! I knew it was always going to be difficult doing something next door, but I'm pleased with the way our Arena and Convention Centre fits into its historic context whilst still making a strong statement on its waterfront.

Not all new Liverpool buildings had melancholy gestations. The twin towers of the Unity Building at 20 Chapel Street by Allford Hall Monaghan Morris (AHMM) make a dramatic contribution to the Liverpool skyline, and, rather amusingly, also make reference to the dazzle-painting finishes they used to apply to warships at the old Cammell Laird dockyards across the water in Birkenhead. The Unity Building adds an energetic 21st-century 'exclamation mark' to Liverpool's waterfront.

Paul Monaghan of AHMM sees the Unity Building as an important totem of Liverpool's rediscovery of itself:

At last… the Liver Building's status as a symbol of the city's past has been challenged by new developments punctuated by towers that suggest what it is and it could become. Liverpool faced extinction, but turned things around. To do so it has had to be brave and at times brash (as it undoubtedly once was when a mercantile city). Liverpool's revival and the architecture that has been that revival's process and symbol should be celebrated. On any day give me a lively city with the confidence to make some highly visible bad mistakes (amongst a lot more good decisions) than one that has died, with its historic core as a crumbling monument to the triumph of good manners.

However, there are questions. While it is true that tall buildings are always effective – if sometimes crude – measures of a city's vitality, there are many people outside the introverted preservation lobby who question both the aesthetic and commercial sense of tall buildings in Liverpool. One of the most remarkable aspects of the old commercial area, located around the thoroughfares of Castle Street, Dale Street and Old Hall Street, is the consistent height and massing of its great historic buildings. To what good end, critics ask, is this impressive regularity to be transgressed?

Yet the Liverpool City Plan rather cleverly avoids any gross transgression. Liverpool has, to a degree, escaped the worst effects of this craze, both by acquiring new tall buildings of architectural merit and by insisting that they be clustered around Old Hall Street, leaving the impressive 'Midwestern' masses of the rest of the commercial area perceptually intact. As I write, however, several tall-building projects are stalled. In 2009, questions of demand and utility have a booming resonance.

Some of Liverpool's best regeneration is smaller-scale, more intuitive and, in the case of Alma de Cuba, cheerfully and typically blasphemous.

Alma de Cuba is a chaste and prim 1788 Catholic church in Seel Street, now translated into whatever opposites of chaste and prim attract the footballers' wives who crowd the intact high altar with champagne flutes. Alma de Cuba is adjacent to the Ropewalks, a pitch-perfect example of creative reuse. Here, many fine historic buildings have been restored and reinvigorated to a masterplan by Building Design Partnership (BDP), with exciting interventions by the cheerfully irreverent local developer Urban Splash. Tom Bloxham, a founder of Urban Splash, drove me around in his black Mercedes 'S' Class one night. Jostling crowds of party-goers were visible on the car's night-vision system. This on streets that only 20 years ago were desolate and dangerous.

Just down the road, biq architecten of Rotterdam has done a fastidious job of restoration and well-mannered new-build at The Bluecoat Chambers, a superb Queen Anne building of 1717–25. biq, in another example of Liverpool's stimulating ability to cultivate incongruities, is inspired by a Benedictine ascetic, Dom Hans van der Laan. Their supplement replaces the part of Bluecoat's 'H'-plan lost to Hitler's bombs; all the vertical bonds in the new brickwork are in beautiful alignment and the roof is in unpatinated copper. Bluecoat was always the darling of Liverpool's architectural hero, Quentin Hughes; now it is tactfully restored and nicely renewed. It is the grit in the oyster which has helped form a pearl.

The 'Bluecoat Triangle' was the original name of Liverpool's most ambitious development. The triangle was defined by South John Street, Hanover Street and Church Street and its extension as Lord Street. This area is bisected by Paradise Street, and soon the project morphed into the 'Paradise Street Development'. Now re-branded 'Liverpool One', it reclaims and revives the exhausted retail centre. Until the arrival of Liverpool One, this was a wasteland of slick, characterless national retail outlets sitting uncomfortably next to the desperate graphics and presentational improvisations of local stores. In addition, plenty of aching dereliction remained from the Second World War.

Liverpool One has been developed by the Grosvenor Estate (the family property company of the Duke of Westminster, whose Belgrave village across the Mersey in Cheshire gave its name to Belgravia, Grosvenor's best-known development). With a determination – even ruthlessness – born of accumulating dismay, the site was cleared by compulsory purchase. The masterplan by BDP responded to a brief insisting on 'permeability' and the retention, to as a great an extent as practicality allowed, of the old street patterns. The brief also insisted on high-quality materials and the idea that the edges of the site should be animated and integrated into the existing context. This is high-minded stuff by the dismaying standards of conventional and artless malls. Grosvenor claims that Liverpool One reconnects the city to the water; what is certain – less rhetorically, but no less importantly – is that it fills a vast, 17-hectare (42-acre) urban 'hole'.

Liverpool One has a reasonable claim to be the most successful UK development of its size and type and in 2009 it became the first masterplan to be nominated for the UK's top architecture award, the Stirling Prize. One important contribution was a variegated squad of architects working to complement rather than obliterate the historic grain and culture. There are over 30 new buildings in its six different districts. They include department stores, hotels, a park, a bus station, a cinema, car parking and 600 dwellings. Contributing architects include Dixon Jones, Page and Park, Glenn Howells, CZWG, John McAslan, Wilkinson Eyre, Cesar Pelli, Michael Squire and Allies and Morrison.

Not everyone is pleased by the efforts of this stellar équipe. Native Liverpudlian architect Sean Griffiths of FAT Architecture called the result an 'endless Modernist Esperanto of polite retail boringness', but while this may be an attention-getting comment in a characteristic local voice, Liverpool One achieves more pleasing variety than Griffiths allows.

v A Bluecoat window
PAUL MCMULLIN

v Paradise Street construction December 2007
PAUL MCMULLIN

v Chevasse Park from the Hilton Hotel
PAUL MCMULLIN

^ The John Lewis store
PAUL MCMULLIN

^ The Cesar Pelli Building
PAUL MCMULLIN

v South John Street
PAUL MCMULLIN

Many different architectural languages – or, at least, quotations – have been built into it. John McAslan's store for John Lewis, for example, very clearly reflects the landmark Peter Jones building in Chelsea whose original design, by Eric(h) Mendelsohn and Charles Reilly, McAslan had meticulously restored. The angled prow of Pelli Clarke Pelli's One Park West, a residential building, has a unique architectural profile, while Wilkinson Eyre's car park is surely the most flamboyantly sculptural example of that genre since Rodney Gordon's masterpiece in Gateshead. Seen at night, South John Street is not a bleak Alphaville of Starbucks and Gap, but an animated street enlivened by good lighting, canopies, walkways and passarelles. If not yet quite so romantic as Atkinson Grimshaw's moody 1887 painting *Liverpool Quay by Moonlight,* as modern cityscape South John Street achieves a level of visual variety and human scale unusual in comparable developments.

Herbert the Hairdresser, a Liverpool institution now accommodated in Piers Gough's Bling Bling Building in Paradise Street, is quite the opposite of retail boringness and stands in defiance of Sean Griffiths's criticism. Somebody once described Gough as a 'B-movie architect'; it was intended as an insult, but – with his pleasure in glittering effects, knowing kitsch and splashy gestures – Gough would take a positive interpretation.

Asked how to describe the signature, boxy projections on this building (for which no term exists in the architectural vocabulary) Gough responded, 'they are our bling'. He says of his strange jettied-out, gilt-and-glass conceit:

The building is what I wanted to say about Liverpool, a city that has powerfully excited me since going there in the sixties. Unlike the protestant showpieces of hard-working cities like Manchester and Leeds, architecturally Liverpool had the catholic swagger of imported wealth. As for now, I like self-deprecation, but it doesn't work as a building style. So it had to be a lovely mix of smouldering and brash.

The Bling Bling was recently voted Liverpool's favourite new building. Maybe the city does make the architecture after all.

To me, the most important thoroughfare in Liverpool is Hope Street, which has been described by the *Observer* journalist and Liverpudlian Ed Vulliamy as 'one of Europe's great boulevards'. Ye Cracke, John Lennon's haunt, is 'one of the best little pubs in the world', and halfway along it is Walter Thomas's Philharmonic of 1900, one of the best big pubs in the world. An Art Nouveau masterpiece, much of its decorative work was done by students of the university's school of art and architecture. Much of the drinking was, and still is, done by them too.

Because it is so much a part of the city's self-image, Hope Street has itself become contentious. Vulliamy

was dismayed, he told his readers, when he discovered that the old Grade II listed Liverpool Art College building, where his mother used to teach (all Liverpudlians are sentimentalists), was to be converted into either a hotel or a residential refurbishment in a proposed development by the Maghull Group. This would translate beery bohemia into champagne-and-sauvignon-blanc territory. Arguments surrounding this now-abandoned proposal are revealing of a local psychology that still affects all new building in Liverpool. Pride and sentiment struggle for victory in a battle against pig-headedness.

More positively, the street has been resurfaced, much to the benefit of boulevardiers. Furthermore, the Art College buildings are being leased back to the John Moores University, also the patron of Rick Mather's fine new Art and Design Academy, an imaginative serpentine conceit in the shadow of Sir Frederick Gibberd's austerity-geometrical Roman Catholic Cathedral (built, in typically surreal Liverpool style, on the site of an old workhouse).

Liverpool is never less than perplexing and contrary. Not long ago, mentioning 'the future of Liverpool' would have sounded ridiculous. People at the University School of Architecture were seriously advocating urban retrenchment, planned depopulation, reforesting and handing the many bits that did not work back to nature. However, times change; now there are loft-dwellers, not shoeless waifs and beggarwomen. In my youth, the big problem in Liverpool on a Saturday night out was getting nutted by an itinerant drunken yob, or breaking your neck after skidding on pavement vomit. Things

v Hope Street
JOHN STONARD

v The Philharmonic Bar
PAUL MCMULLIN

v The Metropolitan Cathedral of Christ the King
PAUL MCMULLIN

are tougher in 2009 than they were last year, but now the big problem on a Saturday night out is finding somewhere to park your Mercedes-Benz.

Sometimes I think the past and future can look after themselves; it's the present we need to be concerned about. As Frank Lloyd Wright's perpetual truism goes, it's the duty of architects to 'make the most of contemporary possibilities'. After all, as John Lennon sang, 'Tomorrow Never Knows'. And what exactly are Liverpool's contemporary circumstances? A lot and nothing has changed. Paul du Noyer explains that Liverpool is not just where music happens, but why it happens. You could replace the word 'music' with the word 'architecture', and that sentence would still make sense.

There is much still to do. The vista of Liverpool from Lime Street Station, despite a bold new gateway that some find intrusive, is still an incongruous mixture of swaggering magnificence and dismaying tat – and still by no means wholly aligned with EU norms. Still, Lime Street, like the Mersey – like Liverpool itself – is a channel both of hope and despair, and thus typical of the place.

There are no easy answers to questions about Liverpool's future. Much has recently been achieved, but

∧ The Liverpool waterfront at sunrise
PAUL MCMULLIN

much remains to be done. Its glorious heritage and its less glorious problems still present humbling challenges to architects and to citizens. Many new developments are of mediocre quality, but beginning with Albert Dock more than 20 years ago, the glorious waterfront has been consistently and painstakingly improved. A new ferry terminal opened in 2009 and a new museum will open in 2011.

Still, Liverpool remains one of the most romantic – if haunted – cities on earth. Simply to add a worthwhile building to Liverpool's extraordinary catalogue of world-class architecture might be the basis for a significant global architectural competition.

While sitting at a railway station (with a ticket for his destination) at Widnes by the Mersey, a New York minstrel called Paul Simon, returning to London from a Liverpool gig, wrote 'Homeward Bound'. Couldn't he wait to get away? Or had Scouse sentiment got to him? One way or another, the city is inspiring.

Liverpool was and is an education, in every sense. And architecture is its curriculum. That is one thing that is never going to change.

3
TRANSFORMING
THE CITY

Whilst Liverpool was granted a charter by King John in 1207, there are no buildings remaining from that period. However, the pattern of the original seven streets is still apparent (formed by Exchange Flags, Castle Street and Old Hall Street running north-south and Chapel Street, Water Street, Tithebarn Street and Dale Street running east-west). The castle, built on high ground overlooking the original 'pool' to the south was destroyed during the Civil War, and demolished in the 1720's.

It is from 1715 that the story of Liverpool really begins, with the opening of the world's first commercial wet dock in the tidal pool that gave shelter from the fast running river Mersey and its severe tidal range. From this point, topographically the lowest in Liverpool, the city expanded in every direction. Significantly, warehouses and merchants dwellings were built south of the tidal pool, on former heathland, enabling the gradual expansion up the hill to the sandstone ridge that forms a natural amphitheatre. These warehouses and houses were frequently built as one structure- house and warehouse in one- and constructed initially along the routes that defined the field boundaries. The long, straight streets were perfect for rope-making, and in addition to warehousing and chandleries, the area became a centre for the manufacture of ropes for shipping. This area is known today as Ropewalks.

As the city grew rapidly, the former merchants housing in Ropewalks became less popular and housing courts were built in the area for workers. By the 1830's the merchant class, uneasy in sharing the same district, started to move to the top of the sandstone ridge in the newly laid out Canning area of the city, as well as moving to the outskirts of the city in leafy parkland areas such as Cressington, and across the river at Rock Park and New Brighton. At the same time, the original seven streets were added to, and became the financial and commercial area for the city, separated from Ropewalks by the Old Dock. During the early decades of the 1800's, the eastern fields and areas of lime kilns, outside of the city boundary, were rapidly absorbed as the city grew and eventually the plateau of Lime Street, with its memory of former industrial activity, became the civic and cultural quarter for the city.

The huge growth in residential population coincided with the expansion of the port, and the Mersey was reclaimed to provide new docks and warehouses, such as the Albert Dock, and the site of the original tidal creek disappeared under new warehousing. The new docks were built to the north and south of the original pool, allowing for characteristic terraced housing for workers to climb the ridge and occupy the hinterland, radiating out from the site of the old dock and the river itself. Whilst some of the areas created were built in a hurry and share very strong cohesive elements, the continuous over-layering and re-development in more established parts of the city has led to a variety and richness that is a Liverpool trait.

These historic layers are crucial to place-making, and understanding them has been an essential requirement for all the recent regeneration of the city. These historic layers are crucial to place-making, and understanding them has been an essential requirement for all the recent regeneration of the city.

The case studies featured in this chapter have been divided into various categories, but it is clear from even a cursory glance that the various projects share common characteristics and that the classifications could be seen as somewhat arbitrary.

Context is a key consideration that is shared throughout the case studies. Like all cities, Liverpool has characteristics which help define it as a specific place, an identity that is different from others. Liverpool has its own personality, a particular feel – it is an 'edgy' city, sometimes less than comfortable, brazen and showy. Whilst design guidance is available both nationally and locally, there is a danger that a strict adherence to design orthodoxy at the expense of a radical approach could dilute quality and promote a bland, universal townscape. Design principles and a maverick approach are both encouraged in Liverpool, and this is explored in the case studies.

The other important commonality in the various case studies is the importance of heritage. Unlike other cities in the UK, with very few exceptions, Liverpool is a World Heritage Site. Most of the city centre is either within its boundaries or within the buffer zone, and this has imposed another layer of policies and guidance that must be considered as part of the design process. The heritage lobby is strong in the city, and there has been opposition to many of the projects in the following sections. Relationships with formal heritage bodies such as English Heritage and UNESCO are strong and many schemes have benefitted from a partnership approach at pre-application stage. The City Council and the private sector have welcomed the contributions made by these bodies in bringing a further degree of analysis and support for high quality development, and a level of understanding that is essential in delivering contextual and relevant design.

Many of the schemes here are conversions of historic buildings, seen as just as important as new build in a city that is rich in heritage. Heritage provides a further level of assessment, and a finer grained approach to the design of new build and of conversion. Liverpool City Council, English Heritage and a number of other agencies have worked in close partnership on the Historic Environment of Liverpool Project (HELP), a unique long-term strategic collaboration which aims to promote and protect the city's rich historic character in a period of radical change. The result has been better understanding and heightened awareness of Liverpool's historic environment , better management of change, and the development of closer strategic working relations between the partner and organisations.

> 'Penelope' on Wolstenholme Square by Jorge Pardo
PAUL MCMULLIN

^ The Strand
PAUL MCMULLIN

PUBLIC REALM

For almost 30 years from the 1960s onwards, Liverpool was subjected to a series of urban experiments and failed projects that led to the fragmentation of its townscape – and the results of these can still be seen in certain places today.

< St Peter's Square
JOHN STONARD

^ Pier Head Canal Link at dusk
PAUL MCMULLIN

Perhaps none were as damaging as the Shankland Plan of 1965, which proposed 'streets in the sky' in order to separate pedestrians from the massive new urban-motorway infrastructure being planned. On listening to Graeme Shankland present these proposals, journalist Simon Jenkins later wrote that it was like being in the room with Arthur 'Bomber' Harris, the RAF Air Vice Marshall who had unleashed the 1,000-bomber raids on Germany in the Second World War. Shankland's plan, illustrating areas of 'obsolescence', shows vast swathes of the city centre as fodder for the demolition ball. Whilst the elevated walkways proposed were quickly recognised as divisive, the Shankland Plan also delivered some of the first pedestrianisation schemes in the UK, much copied in other cities.

As part of its approach to regenerating the city in the late 1990s, Liverpool City Council and Liverpool Vision produced and adopted two key documents on the public realm: the City Centre Movement Strategy and the Public Realm Implementation Framework. These strategic documents ensured that the public realm would act as a linking element in all new development schemes, providing a high-quality framework and a cohesive palette of materials.

< The 'Pavillion
on the Park' by
Studio Three
Architects
PAUL MCMULLIN

< Liverpool One
Water feature
PAUL MCMULLIN

> Campbell Square
JOHN STONARD

∨> Liverpool One
   steps
   PAUL MCMULLIN

The use of high-quality street surfacing, the creation of
new squares and the rejuvenation of existing spaces,
and a strategic approach to the public realm throughout
the city centre are helping to improve the legibility of
the city. The approach is based on simplicity of palette
and subtle changes in tones and dimensions. Granite
and yorkstone have been adopted throughout the city
centre in order to ensure continuity and cohesiveness.

New elements have been added to existing spaces in
order to increase activity. The Pier Head, for example,
now has a new canal as a fundamental part of its
public-realm scheme. Around this canal, there are
amphitheatre-type places to sit, whilst elsewhere at Pier
Head there are larger areas for events and a riverside
walk offering views of the Mersey. Furthermore, Pier
Head forms just one of a whole sequence of new public
spaces along the waterfront, ranging from the large
piazza at King's Waterfront and the Arena to more
intimate areas with bars and restaurants around the
canal basin at Mann Island.

New squares have also been provided in other areas
of the city. In Ropewalks, the long east–west streets
linking the waterfront to the sandstone ridge of Hope
Street and the cathedrals have been supplemented by
a series of new spaces, such as Campbell Square, that
run north–south – ensuring that the previously difficult
cross-routes are now easier, and more pleasant, to
navigate.

The gateway scheme at Lime Street Station combines
clearer routes for movement and more peripheral
spaces for sitting and orientation, whilst Hope Street
in the university area now fulfils its role as a linking
element between the two cathedrals, encouraging
greater ecumenical dialogue between them in an
elegant and harmonious manner.

> Pier Head
JILL JENNINGS

The Hope Street Public Realm scheme realised the aspirations of the local community and its clients in delivering a vibrant and exceptionally high-quality streetscape, comprising new paving and lighting, together with the creation of new squares and artwork.

HOPE STREET PUBLIC REALM IMPROVEMENTS

Hope Street, Liverpool

**Landscape Architect
and Masterplanner:** Camlin Lonsdale
Construction Value: £2.88 million
Completion Date: July 2006
Project Type: Public realm

Introduction

Hope Street forms a distinctive and unique environment, which links Liverpool's main cultural, educational and Georgian quarters and makes a powerful linear connection between the city's two iconic cathedrals. All the city's higher education institutions, the Liverpool Institute of Performing Arts and the Liverpool Royal Philharmonic have major facilities on or around Hope Street. It also hosts a significant residential community and a wide range of commercial interests, including some of the city's best hotels, restaurants and bars. Much of its 1 km length lies either within or immediately adjacent to three of Liverpool's 35 Conservation Areas, with more than 40 Grade II* and Grade II listed buildings on the street's immediate frontage.

The Hope Street Public Realm scheme realised the aspirations of the local community and its clients in delivering a vibrant and exceptionally high-quality streetscape, comprising new paving and lighting, together with the creation of new squares and artwork.

It is an innovative example of public-realm design in a sensitive historic environment, developed in partnership with the local community and public and private sectors. It provides an example of a scheme that is 'owned' by the community, represented here by HOPES, the Hope Street Association, with a seamless joint-client role performed by Liverpool City Council and Liverpool Vision.

Client's Brief

During the consultation phase for Liverpool's Strategic Regeneration Framework the area was repeatedly identified as one needing attention, with a range of community representatives and interests making clear that it was not meeting their aspirations. Liverpool Vision and the council worked with the community and funders over several years to make the initiative a reality.

The intention was for the scheme to provide a tangible set of benefits to all key stakeholders using the street, both now and in the future – including residents, businesses, community organisations, visitors, investors, students and academics. Proposals were to focus on improved pedestrian/vehicular movement, environmental quality, functionality and safety, by:

- maximising Hope Street's strengths as a unique visitor destination and business location of regional and national significance;

- safeguarding current and future patronage of existing regionally/nationally significant cultural facilities;

- reinforcing the area's investment potential;

- facilitating improved linkages and movement to/from the city core along key corridors – for example, Duke Street;

- safeguarding and adding value to other recent investment in the area (e.g. Metropolitan Cathedral Plaza, Hope Street Hotel, etc.);

- improving feelings of safety/security for all users;

- delivering improvements in time for the city's tenure as European Capital of Culture in 2008.

∧ Suitcases on Hope Street
PAUL MCMULLIN

∧ Paving detail
JOHN STONARD

Design Process

In early 2003, urban-design consultants Camlin Lonsdale were appointed to produce a feasibility study and outline proposals. A steering group was also formed with 16 representatives from key stakeholders and the local community – as was a project team comprising Liverpool City Council, Liverpool Vision, the consultants (and, later, the main contractor) to drive the project forward.

A two-day public exhibition was held at the Anglican Cathedral in November 2003 in addition to extensive consultation with the local community, residents' groups, businesses, cultural and creative facilities, and local and national politicians. This proved crucial in finalising design options, construction programme and methodologies with the steering group.

It was vital to both the City Council and Liverpool Vision that the proposals were of the highest design quality, and accorded with the City Centre Public Realm Implementation Framework. The unique character of Hope Street was to be enhanced, traditional details replicated and any furniture was to be bespoke and handcrafted. The scheme was to be pedestrian-friendly, with wide footways and generous crossing points. A series of spaces along the thoroughfare was identified, with these to be designed as squares where people could stop and enjoy the vitality of the area. It was a requirement that the design be adaptable, in order to allow the street to be used for events, and that it should be of a long design life and cost-effective to maintain and clean.

By spring 2005, the final scheme designs meeting all aesthetic, economic and technical requirements were completed, and applications were submitted to public-funding bodies.

The key components of the final design were:

- the realignment of the road to achieve a dignified relationship with the street's architecture, with a general principle of increasing footpath widths where possible;

- the creation of a centrepiece, with a shared surface and public space named 'Philharmonic Square'. This is attractively paved in a chequerboard of green granite, which provides a rich 'carpet' running across the street, slowing traffic and providing a stunning entrance for theatregoers as they cross to the Philharmonic Hall;

- the creation of 'Mount Street Triangle'. This space has a special *genius loci*, capitalising on the location of Hope Street along a topographical ridge and allowing views down to the River Mersey and Wirral peninsula. Paving here is deliberately elevated in order to accentuate the vantage point and provide a location for a popular sculpture depicting the suitcases of illustrious residents, past and present;

- the retention of existing historic paving and the inclusion of new, matching Yorkstone paving throughout in order to give a seamless mix of old and new. Bespoke corner details ensured that each individual piece of stone was separately scheduled to provide a robust design that fits with the character of the Conservation Area;

- the removal of extraneous signage and street furniture;

- the provision of new high-quality, bespoke bronze benches.

Funding was confirmed from the Northwest Regional Development Agency (NWDA), Liverpool City Council and the Homes and Communities Agency (formerly English Partnerships). The project was implemented

^ Hope Street looking towards LIPA and Anglican Cathedral
LCC

by Aggregate Industries, one of the contractors participating in the 'framework' set up to construct works for the City Centre Movement Strategy. Early contractor involvement allowed for the refining of construction details and better control of the final cost.

Project Evaluation

Quality of design/materials and attention to detail were the client-team's highest priorities, and they have been recognised by the Commission for Architecture and the Built Environment (CABE) and in various national design awards. The scheme represents a best-practice approach – from community involvement through to design development, procurement strategy and construction.

The improved thoroughfare was opened with a celebratory day of street entertainment – the success of which has spawned the annual Hope Street Festival, with dance and theatre in the street; the Liverpool Restaurant Group's Food and Drink Festival; the Royal Liverpool Philharmonic Open Day; and further activities organised by HOPES.

Linking the two cathedrals, the street has religious significance and was recently chosen as the location for a statue by Stephen Broadbent celebrating the life and work of former Bishop of Liverpool, David Shepherd who together with Derek Warlock, the former Catholic Archbishop, worked tirelessly for local community cohesion in the 1980s and 1990s.

Hope Street is an ever-popular daytime and evening location, with pavement cafés, restaurants and bars – as well as its theatre and concert venues – all thriving in the enhanced public realm. There is always vibrant activity to be found here, whether it is a rush of theatregoers packing into the Everyman, a gaggle of students celebrating academic success or the many who enjoy strolling this pleasant street, absorbing its marvellous architecture and atmosphere.

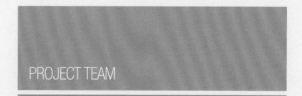

PROJECT TEAM

Client: **Liverpool City Council in partnership with Liverpool Vision**
Client Project Management: **Highways Project Team, Transportation, Liverpool City Council**
Landscape Architect and Masterplanner: **Camlin Lonsdale**
Main Contractor: **Aggregate Industries Ltd**
Quantity Surveyor: **Mouchel Parkman**
Engineer and Project Manager: **Mouchel Parkman**

> The brief was to deliver a simple, clear route to the station, formed from a limited, high-quality palette of granite and Yorkstone.

^ Lime Street station
JOHN STONARD

LIME STREET GATEWAY

Lime Street Railway Station, Liverpool

Architect:	Glenn Howells Architects
Construction Value:	£3.4 million
Completion Date:	April 2010
Project Type:	Public realm

Introduction

Liverpool Lime Street Station is the main gateway to the city, and one of the finest Victorian railway stations in the UK. However, Lime Street's station frontage, with its huge double-span arches, had previously been hidden behind a series of buildings, the latest of which consists of a 13-storey tower and a parade of single-storey shops dating from the late 1960s. This has severely restricted access to the station, and also presented an unappealing introduction to the city.

This public-realm project replaces the existing situation with a series of steps and slopes, inspired by the efficient simplicity of the adjacent William Brown Street cultural buildings. The scheme provides a very legible environment, maximises access and also allows for orientation and meeting areas through the provision of 'seating steps'. Although a decision was made early in the process that the scheme would be based on movement and that physical and visual clutter would be minimised, public art has been an integrated part of the proposals – and a competition was held to choose a designer for this element. The resulting paving surface and glass etchings, based on the theme of transatlantic travel, are both simple and contextual, and complement the limited overall palette of materials with an understated approach.

Client's Brief

The original brief for Lime Street Station approach was based on the provision of a new tower to replace the existing 1967 Concourse House, with associated public-realm improvements. Although the tower was designed, and gained planning permission, financial constraints were such that it could not be constructed.

The subsequent brief was to deliver a simple, clear route to the station, formed from a limited, high-quality palette of granite and Yorkstone. The scheme should allow for ease of pedestrian flow, so that people could move through the area at peak times, but also offer opportunities for pause, orientation and meeting for new visitors to the city. The partnership was particularly keen to provide a public realm that was contextual and sympathetic to the highly graded listed buildings within the locality, which is also a Conservation Area and which lies within the Liverpool Maritime Mercantile World Heritage Site. The arched roof of the station was identified early on as a key visual element that could assist in the design, and this helped to define the overall form of the public-realm works.

Design Process

Liverpool and Manchester shared the first commercial railway line in the world, with Edge Hill Station – opened in 1830 to the east of Liverpool – a contemporary of Manchester's historic Liverpool Road terminus. Originally, passengers were physically lowered in carriages from Edge Hill to the city centre at Crown Street down a steep gradient. It was only in 1836 that a railway station was provided at Lime Street, with a monumental Neo-Classical screen in blonde sandstone, designed by John Foster Jr, to Lime Street itself. Following the rebuilding of the station behind this façade in 1850, the present terminus was constructed in two phases, in 1867 and 1879. The building has a double-span roof (the first of these hidden by the original Station Hotel) and comprises a series of arched openings fronting Lime Street, with a cast-iron and glass roof over the train shed that curves in plan.

The rows of shops that, in some form, have always fronted the station may have provided services to travellers, but they also led to difficulties in accessing the station. This has always been exacerbated by the change in level from the station concourse to Lime

^ Exterior view CGI
GLENN HOWELLS ARCHITECTS

Street, which required steep steps. The drama of the station arches and the sense of arrival were lessened by the prosaic and confusing access arrangements, contrasting with the monumentalism of the train shed and St George's Hall opposite.

The original intention had been to demolish the late 1960s Concourse House tower and replace it with a larger, but more elegant, tower in order to 'hold' the corner of the station arch and complement the public-realm scheme. Whilst the design was completed by Glenn Howells Architects, it proved unviable owing in part to protracted negotiations with the owners of the neighbouring shops and rising costs. However, the partners remained committed to securing a much-needed and improved station access, and commissioned Howells to revisit the public-realm element originally designed by Urban Initiatives. At the same time, the public art design, produced by Simon Faithfull following a competition, was confirmed and the artist commenced his travels to record the journey from Liverpool, UK, to Liverpool, North America. Over 100 of these images have been etched into the station's paving and upstands, and visitors can follow Simon's journey as they move through the space.

Minimal planting, provided by means of the necessary retaining works to the structure of slopes and steps, lends an urban appearance to the scheme, and the stone seating-steps provide informal rest areas. Disability access was a strong design driver and a key part of the brief, and this has been delivered through the introduction of sloping routes and mechanical lifts.

Project Evaluation

The Lime Street Station Approach scheme has provided the city of Liverpool with a new transport gateway that is contextual, efficient and easy to use. The simple palette of materials is robust and entirely fitting for this area of the city centre, complementing the historic surfacing and building materials of the cultural quarter to the north west of the station within the William Brown Street Conservation Area. Planting has been deliberately kept to a minimum to avoid an overly fussy appearance and to allow the fine architecture of the station itself – and of St George's Hall, opposite – to dominate the area.

The scheme allows for much improved access to the station, allowing users a real choice of direction upon arrival for the first time.

PROJECT TEAM

Client: **Liverpool City Council/Homes and Communities Agency (formerly English Partnerships)/ Liverpool Vision/Network Rail**
Architect: **Glenn Howells Architects**
Main Contractor: **Balfour Beatty**
Quantity Surveyor: **EC Harris**
Structural Engineer: **Martin Stockley Associates**
Services Engineer: **BDSP**
Project Manager: **Glenn Howells Architects**
Public Art Consultant: **Simon Faithfull**

Ropewalks has been transformed over the last decade, with many new developments created around a revitalised network of streets and spaces.

ROPEWALKS ACTION PLAN AND FRAMEWORK

Ropewalks, Liverpool city centre

Architect: BDP
Construction Value: £16.5 million
Completion Date: June 2004
Project Type: Public realm

Introduction

The district now known as 'Ropewalks' was previously simply the derelict and run-down area between Bold and Duke Streets in Liverpool city centre. It was once an important part of the city's economy, and its collection of warehouses, grand merchants' residences, factories and terraced houses, built around the location of the Old Dock, stands as a reminder of Liverpool's maritime past. Much of the street pattern and built fabric is the same today as it was 200 years ago, and the long, narrow streets – which at one time were used for rope-binding – are still the defining characteristic of the area.

The Liverpool Ropewalks Partnership was formed in October 1998 to manage a comprehensive programme of investment in Ropewalks, funded primarily through European Union Structural Funds. The Duke Street/ Bold Street Integrated Action Plan (IAP), prepared in October 1997, set out three inter-related programmes of projects around the themes of: Development, Training Employment and Business Support, and Public Realm. Its fundamental aim was to bring derelict buildings back into use, facilitate new development by attracting private investment, ensure that local businesses and residents benefited from that investment, address environmental degradation and poor visual appearance, and improve pedestrian linkages with new and improved public spaces.

The programme came at an exciting time for Ropewalks. Amongst the dereliction, there already existed clusters of creativity, with the large, neglected industrial buildings being ideal for artists' workshops, temporary galleries and recording studios. Concert Square, created by Urban Splash in 1994, was a creative hub in the centre of Ropewalks, and it is surrounded by new bars, apartments and artists'

workshops. The new square established the principles for the use of space in Ropewalks, creating new spaces and routes to draw people into the heart of the area. By the late 1990s Ropewalks was rapidly gaining a reputation as an artistic, cultural and trendy new quarter of the city centre.

Client's Brief

The poor environmental conditions existing in Ropewalks in the 1990s were a major barrier to investment. Improvements to the public realm were needed to demonstrate confidence in the long-term future of the area to potential investors. The improvements needed to be comprehensive and to encompass hard- and soft-landscape measures, both in streets and in spaces. Existing spaces, such as Wolstenholme Square, were to be improved and new spaces, such as Ropewalks Square and St Peters Square, created.

The public-realm works were intended to create the conditions for a wide range of new mixed-use developments by opening up the area and enhancing public access. The location and timing of specific schemes were intended to ensure a direct link with the overall development. This would result in private investment projects being triggered by specific public-realm schemes during the course of the programme.

The projects were intended to:

- maintain and encourage a mix of uses;
- be legible, negotiable, vibrant and active;
- design out crime;
- create clear, safe linkages between nodes of night-time activity;
- create more 'transitional' spaces – places that are neither street nor building but which blur

the distinction, creating vibrancy and allowing surveillance. Shops, bars and restaurants should be allowed to provide outdoor seating and encourage 'colonisation' of these zones;

- turn the streets back into streets, rather than retaining them as predominantly traffic routes.

Design Process

The dual objectives of the public-realm programme were to improve the physical environment and to make the area a more attractive place for private-sector investment. A Public Realm Handbook was prepared by BDP for the Ropewalks Partnership; this set out a number of strategies relating to public art and streetworks, lighting, transportation and parking; and guidance on issues such as materials, emergency access, refuse collection, landscaping, signage and maintenance.

In general terms, the Ropewalks public-realm programme comprised three major elements:

- Redesign of all roadways and footpaths using high-specification materials and items, including new street lighting and street furniture.

  The materials were chosen to enhance the specific character of the area, whilst being simple and durable. Granite setts were specified for the carriageways of the narrow streets in order to reflect the historical surroundings, the original materials used, and to suggest pedestrian priority. Yorkstone was used for footpaths, in combination with granite kerbs. Street furniture, soft landscaping and lighting were to be creative and innovative in their design.

- The acquisition and demolition of strategically located buildings in order to create a series of new public spaces.

- The long, narrow streets of Ropewalks run in a north–south direction, down a gradient towards the site of the Old Dock. The lack of side streets meant that there were few opportunities to walk across Ropewalks in an east–west direction. In addition, the area was very densely formed, with comparatively few spaces in which to stop

and enjoy the surroundings. By creating a coordinated network of new spaces, people would be encouraged to walk across Ropewalks and discover new parts of the district. Buildings were purchased by the Ropewalks Partnership and demolished in order to create new routes and spaces, which cut across the area.

- A strategy for public art and the installation of new major pieces of public art.

  This was intended to highlight key features and improve orientation. The artists and designers were required to collaborate closely on the proposals for the fabric of the area. Competitions were held to appoint artists for specific pieces. New artworks in Ropewalks include the 'Chinese Arch', a gateway feature for Liverpool's Chinatown; 'Metroscopes' opposite the FACT Centre (Foundation for Art and Creative Technology), which consists of five LED displays revolving around steel posts; and 'Penelope', a vibrant, colourful installation intended to complement the surrounding night-time activity in Wolstenholme Square.

A consultation period was undertaken on the Public Realm Handbook, including a series of workshops involving Liverpool City Council departments and local partners. The programme was completed in 2004.

Project Evaluation

Ropewalks has been transformed over the last decade, with many new developments created around a revitalised network of streets and spaces. Many people have been attracted into the area – drawn by apartments, bars, restaurants, clubs and offices. There is a growing residential community, and the office developments have introduced daytime vibrancy. At night, Ropewalks is full of life, with its bars and clubs bringing thousands of visitors – especially around Concert Square.

The improvements have also increased security and natural surveillance along the new pedestrian routes.

It could be argued that Ropewalks has become a victim of its own success. As interest from investors,

∨ Concert Square and Wood Street
PAUL MCMULLIN

∨ Concert Street link from Bold Street
PAUL MCMULLIN

∧ Seel Street
PAUL MCMULLIN

∨ Paving Details
JOHN STONARD

∨ Paving Details
JOHN STONARD

< The 'Banksy' cat (or is it a rat?) on the former
White House Pub at the top of Duke Street.
PAUL MCMULLIN

∧ View from St Peter's Square
PAUL MCMULLIN

∧ Rear of FACT / top of Fleet Street
PAUL MCMULLIN

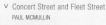
∨ Concert Street and Fleet Street
PAUL MCMULLIN

developers and speculators increased, opportunities
were spotted by speculators to make quick profits,
and the number of planning applications increased
for inappropriate, poor quality schemes. In addition,
the artistic community have been gradually moving
elsewhere as rents increase and buildings are converted
to commercial uses. Liverpool Vision and the City Council
commissioned Jones Lang LaSalle and BDP to complete
a Supplementary Planning Document in 2004 to protect
the special and unique qualities of Ropewalks, whilst
stimulating investment in the remaining development
opportunities in the area. Pockets of neglect remain,
however, and the challenge for Ropewalks is to ensure
that the remaining derelict historic buildings are
protected and converted into new, sustainable uses, and
that the streets and spaces of Ropewalks are vibrant
and animated throughout the daytime and early evening
as well as later in the evening. The enhanced public
realm perhaps presents an opportunity for the artistic
community to return to Ropewalks to showcase their
talents and attract the much needed daytime vibrancy.

PROJECT TEAM

Client: **Liverpool City Council**
Architect: **BDP**
Main Contractor: **Dowhigh Limited**
Quantity Surveyor: **BDP**
Structural Engineer: **Henry Boot Construction Limited**
Services Engineer: **Henry Boot Construction Limited**
Project Manager: **Liverpool Ropewalks Partnership**

The programme has changed the way that urban designers and engineers work together in Liverpool, creating streets and squares rather than vehicle-dominated roads.

∧ Church Street / Paradise Street
PAUL MCMULLIN

> Mathew Street and Hard Day's Night Hotel
PAUL MCMULLIN

CITY CENTRE MOVEMENT STRATEGY

Liverpool city centre

Landscape Architects and Masterplanner: Camlin Lonsdale/Urban Initiatives/BDP/2020 Liverpool
Construction Value: £73 million
Completion Date: Ongoing
Project Type: Public realm

Introduction

In order to support Liverpool's regeneration, Liverpool Vision, Merseytravel and Liverpool City Council developed the City Centre Movement Strategy (CCMS) using a 'golden triangle' approach in which movement, development and public realm were all integrated. This £73 million initiative, which seeks to improve access for everyone, has produced major new improvements to spaces and streetscapes within the city centre.

The Liverpool City Centre Public Realm Implementation Framework was developed by Liverpool City Council and Liverpool Vision as a guide to ensure a coordinated, high-quality approach to streetscape design and materials selection. Its use both for public projects and for private developments has ensured a 'joined-up' methodology, leading to a well-defined local character.

Since 2004, the programme has delivered significant streetscape improvements throughout the city. In the main shopping area these have centred on Williamson Square, with its dramatic new fountain; the Cavern Quarter, famous for the Beatles; and the main hub of Church Street, Lord Street and Whitechapel. Major changes have been achieved in the mixed-use areas of Renshaw and Berry Streets, as well as in Tithebarn Street, around Brunswick Street in the business district and in East Moorfields. Street improvements have been complemented with the creation of new civic squares, in which people can sit and enjoy their city.

Client's Brief

Much emphasis within the project brief was placed on identifying what spaces are used for and analysing what attracts people to use some areas but not others. The creation of vibrant spaces with good pedestrian links, shops and cafés at ground level, and sheltered sunny locations has produced new places in which passers-by are comfortable to linger and 'people-watch' while enjoying public art, water features or pavement cafés. Flexibility was considered vital, so that spaces could be adapted to accommodate new uses over time. Simple solutions were considered the best, and designs took every opportunity to ease future maintenance.

All new spaces were expected to take full vehicular loadings, on the basis that this enables events to be flexibly located and removes the need for bollards to channel servicing traffic. The City Council has been committed to reducing street clutter, and all schemes involved a street-furniture audit and were challenged to enable the combining of signage with joint traffic lights and lighting columns.

The projects have sought to include improved lighting in order to widen the length of time that spaces are used. The City Feature Lighting Scheme has illuminated many of Liverpool's most important buildings, while all public-realm projects include innovative lighting – witness the imaginative use of the Mathew Street 'light blanket' to echo the Beatles' song 'Lucy in the Sky with Diamonds', and the use of vertical light-sticks at Berkeley Place.

^ South John Street
PAUL MCMULLIN

^ Liverpool One Bus Station
JOHN STONARD

Design Process

All implementation was led by the City Council, which set up a dedicated multi-disciplinary team of project managers to deliver the programme. This team included professionals from both engineering and urban design backgrounds, which back in 2003 was considered innovative. They worked together in order to ensure that all projects were imaginatively designed and appropriately detailed. This approach was later endorsed in national guidance, principally the Department for Transport's (DfT) Manual for Streets.

All the schemes started with the preparation of effective design briefs in order to enable appointment of the most appropriate multi-disciplinary design teams. 2020 Liverpool, a design partnership formed between the City Council and consultants Mouchel, acted as lead engineering consultant, and landscape architects/ urban designers were appointed as sub-consultants on a competitive basis along with other specialists – for example, lighting designers and artists. The advantage of using a wide range of designers is that it has brought flair and originality to different areas of the city, whilst still working within the Public Realm Implementation Framework. The proposals involved consultation and workshop sessions with a range of stakeholders.

The designs have sought to include bespoke artistic detail and embellishment. The following examples illustrate how new local identity has been created by the development of new features in the landscape:

- The Williamson Square fountain concept was developed by Camlin Lonsdale working with Fountains Direct. It consists of 20 jets of water, which

rise from the pavements to produce a double arch of water to a maximum height of 4 m. The fountain is programmed by its own computer, which allows for two spectacular displays every hour as well as a misting effect. At night the fountain is illuminated by coloured lighting, producing continuously changing patterns.

- Surrounding the fountain, in stainless steel and beautifully inlaid into the granite paving, is a specially written poem – a gift to the city by Roger McGough. The poem, on the theme of water, has been written so that it can be read from any point around the fountain.

  A walk through the square at lunchtime, or during busy shopping periods, reveals people crowding around to watch the water. It causes much delight and entertainment as people of all ages run the gauntlet through the water jets. Every day there are people photographing the square, and these fountain images obviously remain in their memories of visiting Liverpool.

- The bronze seating in Whitechapel was developed under the auspices of the Liverpool Pool project, as an interpretation of the waterline of Liverpool's original tidal inlet on which the city developed.

- At the rear of James Street Station, an ugly external staircase and back alley was transformed by the imagination of Urban Initiatives. A striking new burnt-orange screen wall and trees now brighten up this previously dingy alley and entrance-way.

^ Cavern walks Setts detail
LCC

^ Whitechapel pedestrian area
LCC

Project Evaluation

The impacts of the CCMS programme have recently been evaluated by independent consulting firm Arup. Its study shows a substantial economic impact in terms of new jobs in the city, and inward investment has resulted from the transport and public-realm improvements.

The project has improved accessibility for pedestrians, and, with new lighting, the perception of safety. Further evidence of success is provided by the increase in the number of public events which are staged in the public ream, for example the opening and closing events for Capital of Culture 2008, public art projects like Superlambanana and the annual Mathew Street music festival. In addition, the schemes have received numerous national design and transport awards, including the Landscape Institute Urban Design Award in 2008 and both a national Contructing Excellence and NW Construction Award 2009.

The major strength of the programme is its adherence to the City Centre Public Realm Implementation Framework – ensuring that all projects join up as a coherent whole, creating a new ambience throughout the city centre. The interface with major retail area Liverpool One was especially critical to making it feel part of the city centre 'offer'. The programme has changed the way that urban designers and engineers work together in Liverpool, creating streets and squares rather than vehicle-dominated roads.

These new spaces have demanded an increase in standards of maintenance and cleansing to include gum-removal and regular street-washing, which have enhanced the experience of the city centre for all.

PROJECT TEAM

Client: Liverpool City Council in partnership with Liverpool Vision and Mersey Travel
Client Project Management: Highways Project Team, Transportation, Liverpool City Council
Landscape Architect and Masterplanner: Camlin Lonsdale/Urban Initiatives/BDP/2020 Liverpool
Main Contractor: Balfour Beatty Civil Engineering Ltd/Wrekin construction/Bardon Construction
Quantity Surveyor: 2020 Liverpool
Engineer and Project Manager: 2020 Liverpool/Faber Maunsell Ltd/ Mouchel
Lighting Consultant: Graham Festenstein Lighting Design/BDP/ Faber Maunsell Ltd

77

The urban designers EDAW were charged with creating a distinctive and vibrant space as a new heart for the waterfront. It needed to be a world-class stage for the city to enjoy festivities, host civic events and welcome visitors from around the globe.

^ Pier Head Canal Link
PAUL MCMULLIN

PIER HEAD CANAL LINK

Pier Head, Liverpool

Landscape Architect and Masterplanner: AECOM Design + Planning
Construction Value: £15m for both canal and public realm at Pier Head;
£8m for public realm only
Completion Date: December 2008
Project Type: Public realm

Introduction

The Pier Head, with its famous 'Three Grace' buildings, is the defining image of the city. At 1.6 ha, it forms one of the largest and most important city spaces at the heart of this World Heritage Site and Liverpool's waterfront.

Liverpool's Strategic Regeneration Framework identified improvements to the Pier Head as a key priority. With a range of major initiatives planned, a masterplan was prepared to maximise the benefits of the proposed extension of the Leeds and Liverpool Canal into the city centre, together with a new Mersey Ferry terminal, proposals for an iconic new museum of Liverpool, and the new cruise liner facility.

The project includes the creation of two sheltered canalside basins, which are flanked with granite seating walls, a central lawn, the replanting of Canada Boulevard and the creation of a large events space. The area is paved in high-quality granite and includes an innovative lighting scheme.

The public-realm project, valued at around £8 million, was led by Liverpool City Council and implemented in a combined delivery, with the Pier Head section of the Liverpool canal link delivered for British Waterways by Balfour Beatty Civil Engineering Ltd. Funding came from the Northwest Regional Development Agency (NWDA) and the Merseyside Objective One Programme.

Client's Brief

The urban designers EDAW were charged with creating a distinctive and vibrant space as a new heart for the waterfront. It needed to be a world-class stage for the city to enjoy festivities, host civic events and welcome visitors from around the globe.

On a practical level, the revived public realm was to strike a balance between canal users, those enjoying the public space year-round and the large crowds envisaged for special events.

The proposals needed to respect the World Heritage Site status, and underwent rigorous scrutiny by English Heritage, the local planning authority and a local design review panel. It was important to reintegrate the city's historic statues and memorials into the new design. The council worked closely with the Canadian High Commission over replanting the memorial avenue dedicated to the Battle of the Atlantic. Ninety-five new semi-mature trees were planted, and existing plaques and interpretation carefully salvaged and reinstated.

The palette of materials and construction method adopted standards from Liverpool's Public Realm Implementation Framework. All pavements were designed to take vehicular loadings.

Finally, the work at Pier Head was to be fully integrated with the adjoining mixed-use Mann Island development, also masterplanned by EDAW.

Design Process

In an epic engineering feat, the canal extension has been excavated in front of the 'Three Graces'. While a large portion of the new waterway runs beneath the plaza, it becomes visible at two large open basins separated by an expansive lawn. These three elements echo the scale and presence of the 'Three Graces' within the public realm. The paving, beneath which the interlinking culverts pass, enables unhindered pedestrian access to the river and provides ample space for civic festivities. This stretch of busy waterway brings movement and interest to the waterfront and provides sheltered places to sit, watch the passing narrow boats and enjoy the views. At 650 metres long, this is the first major UK urban canal extension in a generation.

^ Aerial view
PAUL MCMULLIN

^ Narrow boat on the canal
PAUL MCMULLIN

The canal's water level needed to be several metres below the surface of the public realm. This potentially divisive situation has been ingeniously overcome by conceiving the entire space as a gently folded surface, akin to a beautiful piece of origami, fluidly enabling access for all to the water's edge. The crease lines that create these 'folds' run the length of Pier Head, yet seamlessly change their nature as they move through the space. They are highlighted with a warm-toned natural stone chosen to complement the façades of the 'Three Graces', and used for rainwater collection throughout the space. As they approach the canal basins, however, they splay to dramatic effect, creating 'seat-walls' which accommodate the change in level, elegantly morph into flights of steps, then finally reconverge to continue their journey through the space. In addition to being sculpturally attractive, this inbuilt seating is robust and less vulnerable to vandalism than traditional benches. Computer-generated 3D models were used by the design team to cut complex stone shapes with great accuracy and cost-effectiveness using computer numerically controlled (CNC) milling machines. This 'closed the loop' between designer and end product in a successful piece of digital craftsmanship.

Providing a contrast with the pale stone, mid-grey, varied-tone granite paving forms a rich pattern and texture which takes its inspiration from the variety of stone sizes used in the surrounding historic docks. Within the scheme, a gradation of five module sizes is used, with large flagstones in open expanses blending to cobbles in areas requiring an intricate finish – or where the surface is required to take particularly high weights, such as river-wall maintenance cranes. A subtly varied palette of mid-grey granite not only highlights these unit changes to great effect but also masks surface dirt. The end result is a rich patina across the plaza surface, the subtle coloration being brought to life when wet.

The centrepiece of the design is a new lawn surrounding the restored statue of Edward VII, which sits on the central axis of the space between the Cunard Building and new Mersey Ferry terminal. In spring, this provides a dramatic splash of colour with purple crocuses, whilst in summer it is hard to see the grass for people enjoying the sunshine.

An exciting scheme of night-time illumination was developed, with warm white light used in decorative columns along the main thoroughfares and in innovative recessed light fittings within the canal and seat walls to create attractive feature lighting in the basin areas. The space is overlooked by the new museum and the restaurant terrace of the ferry terminal, and provides a wonderful backdrop at night. All equipment was chosen to be energy-efficient and minimise light spillage.

Project Evaluation

The new-look Pier Head is a key highlight when visitors promenade the Liverpool waterfront, and is highly successful in terms of bringing new animation to what was a rather desolate space. The liveliness of the canal – with its boat traffic, rippling water and reflections – attracts visitors to sit in shelter from the wind and enjoy the new spectacle. The new ferry terminal within the space also helps create a vibrancy, with its outdoor café overlooking the river, rooftop restaurant and Beatles Story attraction – as well being the embarkation point for the popular Mersey Ferry.

Among the greatest strengths of the project is the grand scale of the design, which sits well with the majestic 'Three Graces' and the world-famous setting on the River Mersey. And yet, despite this large scale there are also moments for intimacy, tranquillity and reflection – the latter being especially important, given the number of memorials here.

The area is a successful venue for hosting large events for the city as was seen at the final event for 2008 Capital of Culture, when 35,000 people gathered at the waterfront for entertainment and fireworks. Visitors are frequently seen capturing images of this fantastic space as a record of their visit to the city.

PROJECT TEAM

Client: **Liverpool City Council / Liverpool Vision (public realm) / British Waterways (canal link)**
Landscape Architect and Masterplanner: **AECOM Design + Planning**
Main Contractor: **Balfour Beatty**
Quantity Surveyor: **Faithful + Gould**
Structural Engineer (canal link): **Arup**
Engineering for public realm: **20/20 Liverpool**
Project Manager: **Arup**
Lighting Consultant: **Graham Festenstein Lighting Design**

^ Liverpool One, the 'Big Curve' restaurants
PAUL MCMULLIN

A PLACE TO SHOP

Liverpool has always been a 'one-off', with
a distinctive character not limited to the
physical fabric of the city. Nor is the 'feel'
of the place limited to the unique Scouse
accent or the melding of cultures.

< Wall Street
PAUL MCMULLIN

∧ Debenhams Store at the junction of South John Street and Lord Street
PAUL MCMULLIN

Many in Liverpool would describe themselves as Liverpudlians first, and English second: evidence of a peculiar city-state that continues the tradition of older maritime centres such as Venice. This independence is reflected not only in the buildings, but also an approach to personal style – the look of the city includes its inhabitants as well as its buildings and spaces. Shopping is also viewed as a cultural activity and a 'statement'.

Liverpudlians are adept at taking basic concepts and ideas, and giving them a peculiarly 'Liverpool' twist. Those working on the great liners plying their trade from Liverpool to the Americas in the mid-20th century returned with more than just the usual souvenirs. The 'Cunard Yanks' also brought back blues and embryonic rock and roll, which the city then morphed into a unique Merseysound. Similarly, the architecture of the early 20th-century city owes more to North America than continental Europe. However, edifices such as the Liver Building, India Building and Martins Bank, far from being characterless copies are in fact sophisticated adaptations. They are distinctive Liverpool structures – eclectic perhaps, but nonetheless 'of' a specific place.

> Zig Zag Staircase
PAUL McMULLIN

Another form of culture that Liverpudlians have adopted, adapted and reshaped into something they can call their own is fashion. There is a refusal to be anonymous, or to conform to received taste from elsewhere. On summer evenings, the streets of Liverpool are awash with colour – high couture is partnered with low-cost chain-store clothes to form unique outfits that the original designers could not have imagined.

As with clothes, so with architecture: diverse, cosmopolitan and intriguing – but hardly dull. The Bling Bling Building on Hanover Street has been voted by Liverpudlians as their favourite new building, and there is something about its ostentation and brash appearance that makes it entirely contextual. Liverpool One is a new mixed-use development that refused to be designed to the accepted orthodoxy of an internal shopping mall. Moreover, it is not just about the provision of new shops – the project's urban design has reconnected the area with the river once more. In reaching out for, and relating to, the urban grid around it, the scheme is inclusive and yet remains distinctive. In particular, there are hierarchies apparent within the scheme which have different identities, so that it does not read as a single creation but takes a more 'organic' and varied form. The broad Paradise Street, anchored by the dramatic entrance to the new urban park and leisure 'offers', is immediately identifiable as the main north–south route through the scheme, reflecting the width of the traditional 'high street' of the Church Street/Lord Street axis. Other routes are more intimate and serve for local connectivity – St Peter's Arcade, for example, is a new galleria that links Liverpool One with Church Street, but it has a very different feel to that of Paradise Street. Like the people that populate this place, Liverpool One has its own style and is not afraid to be different.

The Liverpool One Masterplan has single-handedly reversed the fortunes of the city by bringing a new social and economic vibrancy to what was 42 acres of derelict but historic buildings at its heart.

LIVERPOOL ONE MASTERPLAN

Core Masterplan Concept
Design Team: BDP/Davis Langdon/Drivers Jonas/WSP Group/Waterman Partnership/Tenos
Construction Value: £650 million
Completion Date: October 2008
Project Type: New-build

Introduction

Liverpool One repairs and reconnects diverse areas of the city centre. It creates a framework for architecture, landscape and lighting design of the highest quality.

The masterplan governing this enormous project takes great care in connecting into the existing fabric of the city, from the intimate spaces of the Bluecoat Triangle to the civic scale of Chavasse Park. One of the major objectives of the masterplan was that the development should help reconnect the city centre with the waterfront, as well as acting as a hub for pedestrian 'navigation' to surrounding areas such as Ropewalks. The major east–west axis marked by Chavasse Park was the site of Liverpool's commercial dock of 1715, from where the mercantile activity of the city originated. Vistas of Liverpool's famous landmarks root the development in the city and provide a real sense of place. The commitment to create individual buildings in the city has been fulfilled, with appropriate architects being selected for each site within the masterplan.

Liverpool One has breathed new life into the heart of the city.

Client's Brief

By the late 1990s, following decades of decline, Liverpool stood a lowly 17th place in the national retail ranking – a sad reflection on a once-great trading metropolis. Liverpool City Council's research over this period defined the city's plight, highlighting potential demand for almost 100,000 m² of prime retail space. This retail-led capacity formed the backbone of the Paradise Development Area brief, launched by the council in August 1999.

Competing against over 30 national and international submissions, the Grosvenor-led team was appointed as the city's development partner in early 2000, and commenced detailed masterplanning of 17 ha of the city centre. The ambition, agreed by all parties from the outset, was to respect the urban fabric and to create an environment of open streets, individual buildings and places of special character.

The brief evolved over the four-year life of the masterplan (prior to the final planning submission in February 2004) to incorporate 140,000 m² of retail space; 21,000 m² of leisure; over 500 residential units; two hotels; 3,250 m² of office space; a bus interchange; 3,000 car-parking spaces; and a 2.2 ha public park. Critically, the objective of the masterplan was to integrate all of these uses whilst respecting the grain of adjacent urban quarters and encouraging natural movement between existing districts: the main retail area, Ropewalks, the business district and the waterfront.

Design Process

The Liverpool One project has been a remarkable story of collaboration across many teams and professions. In total, some 22 architectural practices have participated in the concept design of the buildings. Within BDP alone, 13 distinct teams have worked across the architecture, landscape and lighting professions on the project's masterplanning, concept design and lighting strategy.

As defined in the masterplan, 22 individual sites were created across the five urban 'quarters', containing some 40 buildings in total. Through a considered

^ Aerial view of Liverpool One
PAUL MCMULLIN

selection process, a range of local, national and international teams was appointed to develop the concept designs for each site – each with a comprehensive dedicated brief prepared by Grosvenor and the masterplan team.

These briefs defined the footprint, function, massing, materiality and overall objective for every building in the context of the wider masterplan. Each building was defined as either 'landmark', 'significant' or 'background', in order to establish its place in the hierarchy of the overall composition. Each concept team was responsible for taking their design through RIBA Stages C and D (Outline to Detailed Proposals) and through to planning approval. Owing to the 'hybrid' nature of the planning applications (some buildings fully designed, with the majority still at outline stage), the majority of the submissions were approved under reserved matters by the City Council.

At the heart of the design-development process were the weekly workshops led by Grosvenor and the masterplan team and attended by the concept teams, representatives of the city, the contracting team and key consultees such as English Heritage.

Fundamental to the setting of the new buildings and the linking public spaces was the creation of high-quality public realm across the site. The masterplan also defined the creation of a major new public park in order to form the centrepiece of the 17 ha Liverpool One development, replacing the largely under-used Chavasse Park.

The design philosophy determined that the new park should create a green oasis, in contrast to the surrounding 'hardscape' of the city centre, with the ability to accommodate a range of changing outdoor seasonal events. In addition, the park had to be accessible on a 24-hour basis for the enjoyment and recreation of all. In response to these requirements, the main amenities of the park comprise a 'Grand Lawn', richly planted terraced and walled gardens, sites for beautiful pavilion buildings, sheltered seating, semi-mature coniferous and deciduous ornamental trees, planting and multi-functional paving areas.

To celebrate the historical maritime importance of this part of Liverpool, a large water feature, commemorating the 'Old Dock' of 1715, has been incorporated into the park, and consists of a series of interlinked pools and fountains. Innovative lighting across the entire green space highlights footways and special features; a complex series of sculptural granite stairways and 'bleachers' links the upper levels of the park to adjacent pedestrian squares and streets. The park's design conceals space for some 2,000 car-parking spaces sitting below its public areas and streets, together with supporting technical areas and servicing. The overall result is a dedicated public space, linking the city and the waterfront, and overlooked by active frontages on all sides: a true 'green heart' for the city.

Project Evaluation

Without question, Liverpool One has played a major role in the changing fortunes of the city centre. In the words of the RIBA North West Region Award judges:

The Liverpool One Masterplan has single-handedly reversed the fortunes of the city by bringing a new social and economic vibrancy to what was 42 acres of derelict but historic buildings at its heart. The result is a vibrant and economically successful retail, leisure and mixed-use quarter – an entirely revitalised city centre that now connects properly with the Docks.

Liverpool city centre is now undoubtedly a destination for an increasing stream of national and international visitors alike. Liverpool One has played its part in

^ Liverpool One Masterplan sites
SUPPLIED BY BDP

^ Liverpool One underground Car Park
PAUL MCMULLIN

reaffirming the pride that Liverpudlians rightly have in their city and its heritage.

In so doing, the masterplan has challenged the orthodoxy that new shopping centres need to be internalised malls – and has delivered new streets and spaces that expand the public realm and help create a vibrant and dynamic place rather than a single venue.

Subsequently several awards have recognised Liverpool One as an international exemplar of retail led urban regeneration.

Masterplan:
Liverpool One Schedule of Concept Architects

1	Dixon Jones
2	Page & Park Architects
3, 3A / B	Haworth Tompkins
4A / B / C	Brock Carmichael Architects
5A / B	Stephenson Bell 5a Façade / Hawkins \ Brown
6	Glen Howells Architects
7 / 7A	Haworth Tompkins Brock Carmichael
8	Greig & Stephenson
8 (pavilion)	FAT
9	CZWG Architects
10	John McAslan & Partners
10A	Wilkinson Eyre Architects
11	Squire & Partners
12	Pelli Clarke Pelli
13A	BDP
13B	Allies and Morrison
13C / D	BDP
14	BDP
14B façade	Marks Barfield Architects
15	BDP / Groupe 6
16G	Studio Three
17 / 17A	Wilkinson Eyre Architects
18	Chapman Taylor
19 / 20	ASL
21 / 22	To be appointed
Public Realm 1	BDP
Public Realm 2	BDP
Public Realm 3	BDP
Park	BDP in association with Pelli Clarke Pelli
Water Feature	Gross Max

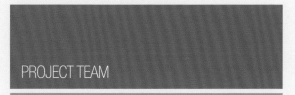

PROJECT TEAM

Client: **Grosvenor Liverpool PSDA Ltd**
Core Masterplan Concept Design Team: **BDP, Davis Langdon, Drivers Jonas, WSP Group, Waterman Partnership, Tenos**
Main Contractor: **Laing O'Rourke and Balfour Beatty**
Concept Architects: **See Schedule below**
Structural Engineer: **Waterman Partnership (Masterplan)**
Services Engineer: **WSP Group (Masterplan)**
Archaeologist: **Oxford Archaeology**
DDA: **Nightingale Associates**
Party wall/rights of light: **Edmund Kirby**
Planning Supervisor: **Capita Symonds**

> PAUL MCMULLIN

The creation of different-
character areas throughout
the Liverpool One scheme
was always intended, and
this organic approach to the
project has delivered a dynamic
development.

ST PETER'S ARCADE

Liverpool One

Architect:	Dixon Jones
Construction Value:	£7.2 million
Completion Date:	October 2008
Project Type:	New-build and public realm

Introduction

Architects Jeremy Dixon and Edward Jones have long
been committed to understanding how cities work, and
have always been interested in arcades. One of the
attractions of the arcade for them is that it is a special
condition of 'the street', in which the designer has
greater overall control than in most other developments
of this type.

Furthermore, there are many memorable examples of
arcades of widely differing scale and ambition. More
recently, however, the arcade has dropped out of
fashion as a retail concept. It is therefore with particular
pleasure that Dixon Jones feels that it has had the
opportunity of looking again at this fascinating building
type.

Client's Brief

When Rod Holmes, the representative of client
Grosvenor, asked Dixon Jones to look at the area that
used to be called Peter's Lane, the brief was simply
to provide retail on two storeys. After examining the
context, the architects came back with the suggestion
that it might be a good location for an arcade – a
typology that would work well with the underlying
premise of the Liverpool One project, which sought
to recreate the traditional pattern of streets and
squares as a means of integrating new areas into the
surrounding city.

Whatever the form, part of the brief was to deal with a
local problem of scale. Historical maps show how the
area evolved around Peter's Lane. Between School Lane
and Church Street, there used to be a large church
and graveyard, called the Cathedral of St Peter, which
was replaced by the present large-scale buildings.
This also explains why it was appropriate at the time
to erect large structures such as the nearby Palatine

^ View of the Arcade
PAUL MCMULLIN

and Russell Buildings. As a result, the two ends of the site have dramatically contrasting scales. At the School Lane end, there are massive warehouse buildings, whereas at the other end the scale is the intimate rear elevation to the Bluecoat. This transition can be happily managed by the way in which the internal nature of an arcade disguises scale changes – at one end the entrance can relate to large buildings and at the other to the smaller ones, and there is an effortless internal transition.

Design Process

Central to the tradition of the arcade is the introduction of natural light into the middle of an urban block. It is possible to review the wide variety of arcade types by looking at their sections and the way in which they introduce daylight, usually via rooflights. One starting point for designing a new arcade was to find an unusual way of introducing natural light into the section. For Dixon Jones, the work of artist James Turrell is a reminder of the magical qualities that can be discovered in reflected daylight. The proposed arcade section used a white quarter-circle vault in order to pick up daylight reflected from a light-coloured external roof surface. The intention was to give the impression that this light came from a mysterious source, and its quality would change according to the position of the sun and the degree to which the sky was overcast. To investigate this lighting effect, the London-based architects experimented with a number of models, taking them out onto Primrose Hill to see how the effects would work.

This lighting idea created an arcade with an asymmetrical section – different from historical examples, which are generally symmetrical. The other ingredient that marks the proposal out as different is the commercial brief to provide a wide pedestrian route, closer in scale to a street. It was felt that an arcade would work commercially only if it could take large pedestrian footfall and had strong retail imagery at each of its two entrances. This is all in the context of the new arcade being a part of a primary shopping circuit starting from Church Street, with its 'cut' through

the former Woolworths building, and linking via Manesty Street to the anchor shopping developments.

The asymmetrical nature of the section is reinforced by having contrasting treatments to the shopfronts on each side of the arcade. Under the clerestory, there are a series of double-height, bow-fronted shop windows using refined bronze detailing and curved glass. Whereas on this side the façade is architecturally controlled, on the other the occupants were to design their own shopfront fit-outs within agreed guidelines, with less architectural control and greater informality. The floor uses a chequerboard of white-and-grey stone as a continuous 'carpet', without marking the structural bays. The arcade route slopes roughly a metre from end to end, giving rise to the well-established effect of false perspective. In one direction the length appears to be increased; in the other, diminished.

At each end, the arcade is entered from a small urban square. At the School Lane end the new square is of unusual proportions and acts as a transition between the arcade, and the new route through to Church Street. Here a tall, polished dark-granite wall encloses two sides of the square and frames the entrance to the arcade with its adjacent shop front. The polished granite reflects the decorated façade of the restored County Palatine Building, as well as having its own internal reflections within the 'fold' of the corner. The 'floor' of the new space has a nine-square grid picked out with lines of dark granite.

Project Evaluation

One of the ideas behind Grosvenor's Liverpool One project has been to have different architects working on adjacent sites in such a way that productive discussions might take place between them.

In the case of St Peter's Arcade the site is shared with architects Haworth Tompkins, and Dixon Jones enjoyed working with the talented, younger practice in evolving the adjacencies along College Lane – in particular the design of neighbouring façades.

^ Arcade detail
PAUL MCMULLIN

^ The Arcade
PAUL MCMULLIN

The underlying idea for the Grosvenor project as a whole has been to provide a controlled level of diversity, so that a visually interesting urban environment can evolve as a natural extension of the historical city. The creation of different-character areas throughout the Liverpool One scheme was always intended, and this organic, seemingly evolved, approach to the project has delivered a dynamic development. The arcade, whilst forming part of the greater Liverpool One development, is unique in this context, and not only looks but feels very different from the other streets within the scheme. The arcade also responds to local context, with an ingenious slot cut into its monumental granite walls to reveal the rooftop lantern of the Bluecoat – a local landmark.

PROJECT TEAM

Client: **Grosvenor Estates**
Architect: **Dixon Jones**
Main Contractor: **Balfour Beatty**
Quantity Surveyor: **Davis Langdon & Everest**
Structural Engineer: **Waterman Group Ltd**
Services Engineer: **Hoare Lea**
Project Manager: **Grosvenor Estates**

Building 13b is the centrepiece of Grosvenor's masterplan to extend and complete the city's retail core and connect it to the Albert Dock. With a footprint of more than a hectare, the block contains – over five levels – some 50 shops, 20 cafés and a cinema entrance.

13B PARADISE STREET

Liverpool One

Architects:	Allies and Morrison/BDP
Construction Value:	£45 million
Completion Date:	Phase I: May 2008
Phase II:	September 2008
Project Type:	New-build

Introduction

Building 13b is the centrepiece of Grosvenor's masterplan to extend and complete the city's retail core and connect it to the Albert Dock. With a footprint of more than a hectare, the block contains – over five levels – some 50 shops, 20 cafés and a cinema entrance. These are organised around a series of stratified public routes, which connect into the surrounding street pattern at a number of levels and which have two distinct 'faces': the urban side on Paradise Street has three-storey shops with a ribbon of cafés above; the park side connects via two bridges to Chavasse Park, facing the Mersey, and is 14 m higher than the level of Paradise Street. Here, the curving geometry of the park is imposed on the form of the block, held by an oversailing 'halo' comprising elliptical building form at high level with canopies, and emphasised by the zigzag glazing. Below this, South John Street offers multi-level shopping linked to department stores at each end.

Between these two sides, a major cross route, aligned with College Lane, rises up from Paradise Street to the park. This 'cut' in the urban frontage holds escalators and a zigzag stair, which leads to a covered galleria, the arrival space for the cinema and its associated cafés.

Client's Brief

Allies and Morrison were appointed by Grosvenor in 2004, following an invited competition to develop site 13b for a planning application and design to RIBA Stage D+ (Scheme Design). The detailed design of the building was undertaken in collaboration with BDP.

The brief was to develop the building within the parameters and constraints of the wider masterplan designed by BDP, and to do so with Grosvenor and alongside Laing O'Rourke as project manager and contractor.

The design has therefore been progressed with close contact between the architects, masterplan architects, client and contractors. Consultation formed a key part in the design development, with stakeholders and Liverpool planners always represented at presentation and design workshops. The scheme was designed as a shell-and-core building only, with flexible retail units at the ground and first floor (mezzanine levels are at second floor) and leisure units (restaurants, cinema entrance, etc.) at third floor (with mezzanine levels at fourth floor). All retail and leisure units had to be designed to be flexible.

13b accommodates most of the basement air plant on its roof, with service risers penetrating the building in several locations.

Design Process

Site 13b is both a building and an urban block. It has two very different sides: firstly, the city side (Paradise Street, Paradise Place and Thomas's Lane), an area of densely packed urban blocks; secondly, the Mersey side (South John Street and Chavasse Park), a world of open space and sea breezes. The character, grain, material and scale of each differs in response to its context.

The uses within Site 13b, as well as its relationship with the public realm, are stratified: three levels of retail below park level, in 'shopping streets'; two levels of leisure above, relating to the park. This unusual section locks naturally into the 'artificial hill' of the new park, built over four storeys of parking; a re-creation of the original medieval castle promontory.

At upper level, the urban block is bisected by College Lane, which cuts across Paradise Street and leads via the zigzag stair and Galleria up to the park. A vertical 'vein' is thus created, connecting the two levels and leading to the grand elliptical curve of the Plateau, known as the 'Big Curve' fronting the park.

^ Level One interior
PAUL MCMULLIN

The building's form results from the masterplan constraints – in particular, the retention of key views towards the Liver Building and the Anglican Cathedral. Its development can be likened to a process of erosion; a fluid, horizontally banded façade has emerged, offering a coherent but appropriately diverse response.

The masterplan and its individual buildings were designed in close contact with the Liverpool planners. Planning parameters were set by the masterplan – building heights, floor areas, strategic views, zones for material and colour. Masonry, robust detailing and a strong 'Classical' order set the character of the urban side of the block, which is dominated by the retail parade on Paradise Street and Paradise Place.

By contrast, the South John Street colonnade is seen as a group of inserted structures 'docked' against the urban block rather than being part of it. It is an architectural element which gathers together stairs, bridges, escalators and canopies, and yet allows them a distinct character.

Above this, the 'Big Curve' facing the park continues the theme of differentiation from the urban front. Like a geode cut to reveal crystal within, its faceted surface reflects the importance of this 'civic' frontage to the park.

This many-sided composition is ordered by the simple continuity of key horizontal bands which run around the block – both its outer envelope and the semi-interior space of the Galleria – unifying the whole. These horizontal strata respond to the diverse orientation and massing offered by the site with a series of distinct volumetric solutions, while maintaining a consistent architectural language.

The main façades are clad with German limestone – Scheinsberger (bush-hammered finish). The stone is cast onto prefabricated concrete panels spanning 8 m between the columns. The secondary façades down Thomas's Lane and at high level on the Galleria are pre-cast concrete panels, with the stone feathered into the concrete at both ends of Thomas's Lane. The 'strata bands' are Portland stone, while the third-floor (Big Curve) level band and floor is Chinese granite. The Galleria roof is a fully welded structural-steel frame sitting on stainless-steel columns, with a lightweight glass roof and aluminium louvres.

The South John Street colonnade is a painted mild-steel structure, incorporating bridges with stainless-steel columns. The upper-level Big Curve comprises predominately zigzag glazing, with a painted aluminium 'halo' supported on folded steel columns at each end.

Project Evaluation

Retail buildings normally generate significant internal heat gains – mostly from people and display lighting. 13b Paradise Street has a car park beneath it, and a computer model simulated the effects of removing the insulation that was to be placed between the car park and the site's retail space. The results showed that the building would operate for most of the year in cooling mode. Therefore, removing the ground-floor insulation meant it would operate as a 'chilled floor' and assist with the cooling process, achieving an element of 'free cooling' and giving a reduction in energy consumption over the notional building of around 10 per cent.

∧ View from the Hilton Hotel of the restaurants on the 'Big Curve' on Level 1
PAUL MCMULLIN

∨ Long Section plan
SUPPLIED BY ARCHITECT

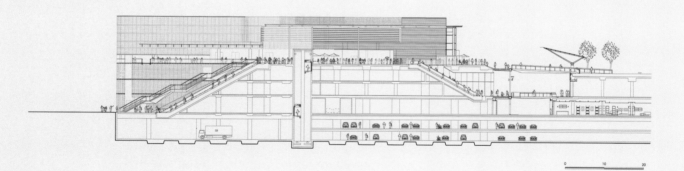

The scheme is fully accessible. All public spaces can be accessed by lift, ramp, escalators or stairs. The zigzag stair is a good example of imaginatively designed safe access: the original design allowed for a straight stair alongside the escalators, but Liverpool's Building Control Department insisted on a change in direction. All the external ramps and sloping bridges have a gradient of no more than 1:21. All levels of the building are accessible 24 hours a day, and the lighting and public spaces are all designed to create a safe environment.

PROJECT TEAM

Client: **Grosvenor Liverpool PSDA Ltd**

Developer: **Grosvenor**

Construction partnership: **Grosvenor and Laing O'Rourke**

Concept Architect: **Allies and Morrison**

Masterplan and Construction Architect: **BDP**

Main Contractor: **Laing O'Rourke**

Quantity Surveyor: **Davis Langdon**

Structural Engineer: **Waterman Partnership**

Services Engineer: **WSP, Birmingham**

Project Manager: **Laing O'Rourke**

Fire Consultant: **Tenos Ltd**

Lighting Designer: **BDP**

Through the innovative use of traditional materials and construction techniques, the architects were able to create the 'jewel-like' projections which so distinguish this building.

BLING BLING BUILDING

Hanover Street and School Lane, Liverpool

Architect: CZWG Architects LLP
Construction Value: £3.5 million
Completion Date: September 2006
Project Type: New-build

∧ Street elevation
PAUL MCMULLIN

Introduction

Grosvenor Estates has developed an exemplary new shopping precinct, based on improved streets, squares and a spectacular park. At the first stage of implementation, a well-known flamboyant hairdresser, Herbert's of Liverpool, relocated its salon and school to the lower half and top floor of this new building on the corner of Hanover Street and School Lane (the other areas of the building comprising office space).

Placed between two exuberant and powerful Edwardian neighbours – the red/orange brick chambers of the Abney Building and the listed Crane Building, incorporating the Neptune Theatre – the new block celebrates views of and from its surroundings, including of the Liver Building, with three major bay windows set into wrap-around curtain walling enriched with deep mullions and transoms. These bays are like chunky golden jewellery on the building, hence its nickname: the 'Bling Bling Building'.

Located in the Duke Street Conservation Area, the Bling Bling Building is bounded by the two streets to the north and southeast and the L-shaped Abney Building to the southwest and south. Hanover Street is an 18 m-wide main thoroughfare. School Lane is only 8 m across at this point, but widens along its length – particularly opposite the listed Bluecoat School. To the southeast, Fleet Street – one of the dramatic, narrow warehouse-lined streets of the Ropewalks area – runs uphill. The site terminates the vista down this long street, its axis not quite on its acute corner but adjacent to it.

Across Hanover Street is a mix of lower buildings, mainly of red brick with stone or terracotta dressing but including an interesting Art Deco faience façade with a zigzag-motif cornice.

Hanover Street is approximately level along the site. However, School Lane falls some 900 mm from its intersection with the former to the Abney Building to the east.

Client's Brief

The client required a commercial building on the basement, ground and six upper stories, covering the footprint of the site.

Basement, ground, first and second floors were to include a prospective mix of retail, restaurant, beauty salon, leisure, education and office uses. The third to sixth floors were to be speculative office space. Later, the hairdresser took the top floor as his own office. The early relocation of a salon and school from a vital site on Paradise Street led to a requirement for a swift planning and procurement process. From initial commission to full planning application was less than a month!

Although a relatively small development, the Hanover Street offices were on the 'critical path' of the whole 17 ha city-centre redevelopment project, as they were required to rehouse existing tenants and release space for subsequent phases of the works. Furthermore, the design process was subject to enormous scrutiny from a significant number of third parties. It was therefore imperative that CZWG Architects produced clear and concise design reports, and the practice made numerous multi-media presentations to the design review panels.

Design Process

Building Form

The entrance to the hairdressing salon and school is from Hanover Street; that to the upper-level offices is from School Lane. This leaves a clear run of shopfront between them, which includes the prominent corner.

The concept for the design was of a boundary envelope patterned with a repeated frame carrying large bay-window elements that responded to the heights and features of the many, varied surrounding buildings. These elements would also clearly express the entry, uses and opportunities of the Bling Bling Building itself. This envelope is made up of 1.5 m-wide by 1.75 m-high

glass panels, radiused to a bullnosed curve on the acute street corner. The curtain walling has aerofoil-shaped mullions: at each vertical/horizontal junction, they are capped with a piece of gold 'mini-bling'. At ground-floor level, planar glazing is inserted into the grid to form the shopfronts. The bay elements responsible for its reputation occur at different levels across the façades of the building.

The bay feature spanning from first to second floor denotes the entrance to the hairdressing salon and its connection to the two levels above, including the school. Its form visually unites these floors at the entrance point with an open, inverted 'U' shape – perhaps denoting a (particularly severe) haircut.

Crowning the façade on Hanover Street is a projecting bay exactly corresponding to Fleet Street opposite, and also angled on the line of that thoroughfare. Its parapet coincides with the penultimate cornice of the adjacent Crane Building. On School Lane, a box bay at third floor level projects out, affording views from up and down the street and to the Liver Building beyond. This bay has an accessible balcony on the fourth floor.

In an inversion of the norm, the corner of the building is a floor lower than the remainder. This gives a great view of the Crane Building cornice from Fleet Street – and a corner terrace is thereby provided to the sixth floor.

The bays are envisaged as large elements of jewellery on the relatively plain façades of the building. They are designed to fit to the grid openings of the elevation, but are made more expressive through three-dimensional surface modelling. The overall effect is of baroque elements at each level of the building, thus entering into the spirit of its Edwardian neighbours in a modern idiom.

Structure and Materials

Inside the Bling Bling Building, a reinforced-concrete structure of columns and stair/lift-core walls supports flat slabs with cantilevered elements. Its flat roofs consist, for the most part, of concrete paving laid on insulation.

Aluminium-framed curtain walling, with tinted glass windows and opaque glass panels, is provided to all elevations. Bays and oriels are clad in a gold-coloured copper-and-aluminium alloy over a steel-and-timber frame, and their window elements consist of clear double glazing in recessed frames. Shopfronts and doors, together with the entrance doors to the offices, comprise single planar glazing.

Project Evaluation

For the main elevation fronting the Hanover Street offices, achieving a 'Very good' BREEAM (Building Research Establishment Environmental Assessment Method) rating within such a confined city-centre site was particularly challenging. Careful glazing specification and the use of exposed structural soffits within the office space allowed the building to be passively ventilated – relying on wind-driven cross-ventilation and night cooling, and thereby achieving high credit scores for the 'Health & Wellbeing' section of the BREEAM assessment as well as reducing the building's CO_2 emissions.

The initial concept for the external envelope proposed high-end materials appropriate for a 'flagship' building which showcased the client's intent, constituting as it did the first element to be completed in the £800 million redevelopment of Liverpool city centre. However, on commencement of the Stage D (architects' Detailed Proposals) work, the client made substantial reductions to the cost-plan budget. Nonetheless, through the innovative use of traditional materials and construction techniques, such as the copper sheeting on a timber substrate, the architects were able to create the 'jewel-like' projections which so distinguish this building whilst delivering the project within budget.

PROJECT TEAM

Client: **Grosvenor**
Architect: **CZWG Architects LLP**
Main Contractor: **David Mclean Contractors Ltd**
Quantity Surveyor: **Davis Langdon LLP**
Structural Engineer: **Arup**
Services Engineer: **Arup**
Project Manager: **Laing O'Rourke**

97

∧ Cityscape sunset
PAUL MCMULLIN

A PLACE TO WORK

Unlike that of other northern cities,
Liverpool's economy has never been based
on the manufacturing industries. Commercial
activity has always been at the heart of
Liverpool's vibrancy and economic success.

< India Building
PAUL MCMULLIN

∧ Matchworks Phase 1
PAUL MCMULLIN

The commercial area of the city, including the Pier Head, is characterised by historic buildings of great architectural richness and ornamentation that are part office and part company brands. They were designed to impress, and are architectural expressions of the underlying wealth and importance of a city that for a lengthy period in the 19th and early 20th centuries was one of the great powerhouses of global trade and finance.

In stark contrast to the grand offices of the shipping lines, insurance agents and traders, Liverpool's commercial heritage also includes its ubiquitous and utilitarian warehouse buildings.

Central to the regeneration of the city, has been the adaptive reuse of these historic structures. Many of the warehouse buildings in areas such as Ropewalks have been converted to a number of new uses. Whilst some may mourn the loss of the industries that used to inhabit these buildings – an inevitable consequence of times of economic decline – others celebrate the ingenuity of conversion and the fact that the loss of original use has not led to loss of fabric. Both the Tea Factory and the Match Factory projects demonstrate that

constant reinvention and an ability to adapt and survive are at the core of Liverpool's success.

The retention of such buildings has also helped to maintain Liverpool's distinctiveness – and new buildings have, on the whole, added to this. The scale of the new-build in Ropewalks, for example, respects the four- to five-storey general heights, and the historic pattern of narrow building plots has been repeated in order to give the same sense of rhythm. The warehouse typology has been influential throughout the city centre as an inspiration for new development, and this has given a sense of continuity and coherence. The simple structure of larger-scale buildings fronting wider streets, with smaller buildings to the rear, has also been maintained – and this has helped to promote hierarchies and legibility. Although new tall buildings have appeared they have been subject to a strong rationale that again emphasises the structure of the city, either adding to the cluster within the commercial core of the city, such as the Unity development at 20 Chapel Street, or marking key 'nodes' or gateways.

Buildings and new urban spaces, like St Paul's Square, demonstrate how to work with the grain of the city fabric and its individual historic buildings in order to deliver places of work that are dynamic and contemporary, and yet which resonate with the city's essential heritage – providing both the comfort of continuity and the excitement of modernity.

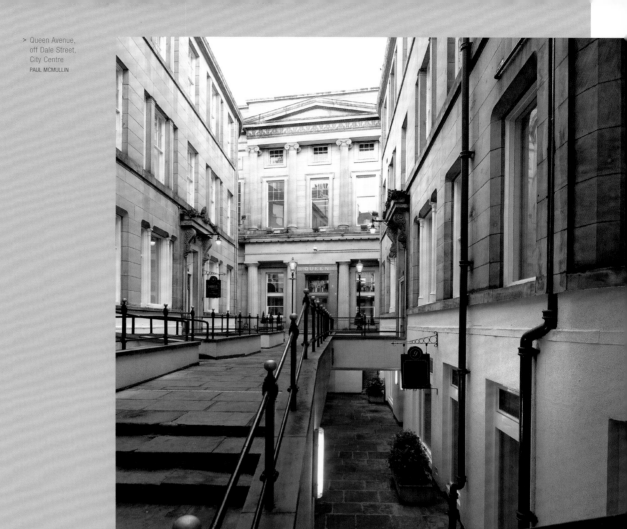

> Queen Avenue,
off Dale Street,
City Centre
PAUL MCMULLIN

> Old Hall Street
PAUL MCMULLIN

The dual towers serve as a powerful complement to the waterfront silhouette of Liverpool's 'Three Graces' at the Pier Head.

^ Unity Building
PAUL MCMULLIN

UNITY, LIVERPOOL

20 Chapel Street Liverpool

Architect: Allford Hall Monaghan Morris
Construction Value: £57 million
Completion Date: December 2006
Project Type: New-build

Introduction

Located immediately northeast of the Liver Building, the Unity development consists of two towers, rising from a podium, which house residential units, offices and retail space. The dual towers serve as a powerful complement to the waterfront silhouette of Liverpool's 'Three Graces' at the Pier Head. At the same time, they have been designed in ensemble with the smaller existing Atlantic Hotel on the plot next door.

As a result of economic stagnation, there have been no new offices built in Liverpool for the last 30 years. The Unity office accommodation sets a new qualitative benchmark for lettable workspace, and is effectively priming a new market for serviced space within the city centre. At the start of construction, the Unity's office component was the largest commercial development outside London in the UK. Amenities for staff and residents in the adjacent tower include a gym, shops, cafés and restaurants, together with the use of the landscaped courtyard around which the podium wraps.

The Unity building's residential component is a response to the huge demand for such accommodation within the city – a fact that was confirmed when 90 per cent of the flats, all privately owned, sold within 18 months of the project's completion.

Client's Brief

The brief was for a mixed-use scheme with approximately 15,000 m² of office accommodation, shops and parking, plus 161 residential units. The site is situated just north of the Liver Building, and enjoys spectacular views of the Mersey and the Wirral beyond.

More practically, this mixed development has responded sure-footedly to major demographic changes in the city, and has set new benchmarks for office accommodation in a traditionally weak letting market. This was also

to be a project which demonstrated that – with imaginative design thinking, shared goals and well-managed collaboration – design-build contracts could produce landmark-quality architecture.

Initially, the commercial viability of the office tower proved challenging as the rental yields within Liverpool proved insufficient to fund new-build commercial space. Liverpool Vision, the City Council and the Northwest Development Agency (NWDA) believed that the mixed-use nature of the scheme was of crucial importance, both to the site and to the wider context of city-centre regeneration. A decision was made to offer a grant to partially fund the office building and 'prime' a new market for modern office space within the commercial quarter. The Unity marks a new commercial frontier for Liverpool. Rents, although higher than previous benchmarks, represented value within a market dominated by older, converted, cellular accommodation.

Design Process

Halfway through the design process on the Unity, Liverpool was made European City of Culture for 2008. Attention suddenly focused on a symbol for the city's renaissance and the design of a new city landmark for the World Heritage Site surrounding Liverpool's 'Three Graces'. The two towers of the Unity building serve as powerful complements to the waterfront silhouette of these famous Merseyside buildings. The towers became symbols of the city's renaissance for its year as City of Culture – not least because the Unity is the first large-scale speculative office provision in decades.

The design of the twin Unity towers therefore needs to be viewed in context, as an important element within the whole city block rather than as isolated structures; their forms contrast with each other, the neighbouring Thistle Hotel and the surrounding business district. Thus, the scheme was designed to achieve a natural,

> Interior view
MCCOY WYNNE

^ External view
MCCOY WYNNE

curving progression inland from the 'Three Graces' on the waterfront to the Atlantic Hotel and, via the office tower with its stepped upper floors, across to the similarly stepped residential tower and up to its terminating stainless-steel penthouse 'pod' high in the sky. This is a scheme which can be read close up as a pair of elegantly unusual towers rising from a clearly defined city block, and from a distance as part of an ensemble of characterful building forms.

Unlike conventionally fashionable, all-glass towers, those of the Unity have imaginatively coloured and patterned cladding panels in elongated 'T' configurations. The slightly more conventional office-tower skin is based on horizontal strip windows and spandrel panels, overlaid with a regular 'hit-and-miss' pattern of projecting vertical floor-height glossy-black panels. Texture is provided on the residential tower using a system of inset and projecting balconies – and on the office-cladding system by the use of projecting cladding panels.

This distinctive patterning explores ideas of scale and urban camouflage, and makes reference to the 'Dazzle' ships that were painted on the Liverpool waterfront during the First World War by Vorticist artists such as Edward Wadsworth. This Dazzle-ship motif/reference informs the colours used throughout the scheme, from balconies (on the residential element) to toilet areas (in the commercial one), the striped residential corridors and the lining of the office-building's entrance lobby.

The residential block was built using tunnel-form construction – a building method which involves the

reuse of apartment-sized steel formwork. The use of in situ concrete for walls and floors ensured good acoustic and fire separation between flats. The office-block floors have long structural spans, made possible by the employment of post-tensioned reinforcement. Worries about work operatives' safety in constructing the penthouse pod on the adjoining tower were allayed by employing a complex, cantilevered temporary-formwork platform, which supported the pour of the main slab. The pod itself was then constructed with a lightweight steel frame. The roof was made from modular prefabricated sections, craned in and sealed up over a three-day period.

Equally innovative was the printed glass within the public areas of both towers: this employed modern computer-printing technology, enabling exceptional colour saturation and accuracy.

Project Evaluation

In this bespoke design-build contract, Allford Hall Monaghan Morris and the client, Rumford Investments, assembled a conventional design team, to which AHMM added Studio Myserscough, who researched and reinterpreted the Dazzle ship designs. The building-design team, main contractor and the major subcontractors were all united in using a computerised central-information and transaction hub which eliminated paper drawings, established audit trails and provided most communication. Although this was a design-build contract, everybody involved was committed to maintaining design quality and exploring new ideas.

^ Dusk view
MCCOY WYNNE

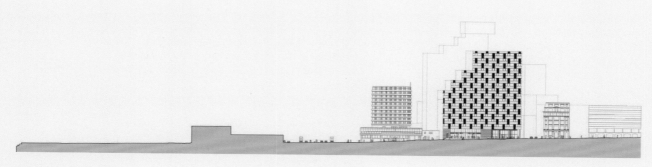

^ Elevation looking north east
SUPPLIED BY ARCHITECT

Component and package development took place after thorough briefing sessions involving architects, subcontractors and the contractor in order to deliver design aspirations at a price that worked. This collaboration proved to be both enjoyable and fruitful for all involved: the working method proved very successful and virtually eliminated the need for the inevitable 'Value Engineering' of each package.

More practically, this mixed-use development has responded confidently to major demographic changes in the city, and has set new targets in the consideration of office accommodation. Apart from stretching construction technologies to their safe limits this is a project which demonstrates that – with imaginative design thinking, shared goals and well-managed collaboration – design-build contracts can produce landmark-quality architecture.

PROJECT TEAM

Client: **Rumford Investments Ltd**
Architect: **Allford Hall Monaghan Morris**
Main Contractor: **Laing O'Rourke Plc**
Quantity Surveyor: **Goyne Adams**
Quantity Surveyor (penthouses): **John Shreeves & Partners**
Structural Engineer: **Faber Maunsell**
Services Engineer: **Hoare Lea**
Services Engineer (penthouses): **Rotary Barrats**
Project Manager: **Mace Ltd**
Landscape Architect: **Kinnear Landscape Architects**
Acoustic Engineer: **Sol Acoustics**
Graphic Designer: **Studio Myerscough**

105

The works undertaken at Matchworks and the new-build Matchbox illustrate how clusters of commercial units in out-of-town areas need not resemble soulless business parks, devoid of character and quality.

MATCHWORKS PHASE II

Speke Road, Garston, Liverpool

Architect:	shedkm architects
Construction Value:	£8.5 million
Completion Date:	March 2008
Project Type:	Combination of new-build (the 'Matchbox') and conversion (the 1948 building)

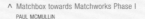

^ Matchbox towards Matchworks Phase I
PAUL MCMULLIN

Introduction

The new 'Matchbox' and the reconstruction of the existing 1948 building formed the second phase of Urban Splash's regeneration of the Grade II listed, derelict Bryant & May Match Factory, started as a concept in 1997. shedkm's involvement stems from the very beginning of this process, and has led to the creation of a new business environment, which, although involving a change of use from factory to white-collar working, has kept the visual impact of the old factory intact.

To drive past the Matchworks en route from John Lennon Airport to the centre of town, one becomes immediately aware of a group of buildings set against a landscaped backdrop, which are entirely different from (indeed, almost at odds with) the standard out-of-town steel-clad 'outlet-village' style developments nearby. A major reason for this is, of course, the quality, style and proportion of the existing Match Factory buildings themselves. However, on closer inspection it can be seen that the subtlety of the architects' interventions has added something that brings a sense of the contemporary and a new vitality to the assembled group of buildings. The all-glass new-build 'Matchbox', set unusually on a diagonal axis, enhances the impact in a thoroughly modern way – as does the massive red portal at the entrance gate.

Client's Brief

The client (Urban Splash, and in particular Tom Bloxham) wanted a strong visual impact on this pivotal city-gateway site. Exactly how the semi-derelict buildings were to be developed was not entirely clear in the beginning. In this respect, the client's needs remained flexible. The briefing process was more a matter of developing uses, as the plan and constraints of the existing shells became more apparent. This was

an interesting period in that, for shedkm, the client's requirements were to be interpreted and built upon gradually, rather than written in a product-specific brief. In a sense this was unusual, but in reality it gave the opportunity for the business plan to evolve naturally alongside initial ideas for how the built form could be adapted.

The regeneration body – Speke Garston Development Corporation – was particularly helpful in accepting, through a series of presentations, this approach. Ultimately, the Matchworks proved itself: from being a factory producing mass-market matches (one of the smallest of objects) it became a business environment accommodating a whole variety of enterprises, ranging from the offices of an NHS primary care trust to a karate studio. Yet, even with such changes, it was still the famous 'Matchworks' – an integral part of Liverpool's history.

Design Process

The design process followed a pattern of evaluation, development, implementation, then construction. At none of these stages could it be said that the design became 'finite' – except in the case of the new-build 'Matchbox'. This pattern is inevitable when working with existing buildings, if their maximum potential is to be realised. Therefore, the pattern of design development for the 1948 building closely followed that of the Matchworks Phase I, whilst the iconic 'Matchbox' stood alone from the beginning like a pavilion set formally against a landscaped backdrop.

The 'Matchbox'

The building was conceived as a three-storey landmark pavilion situated on the Banks Road corner of the site in order to form a highly visible marker for the development as a whole. To enhance the effect, and to

^ The Matchbox
PAUL MCMULLIN

^ Interior of Matchbox
PAUL MCMULLIN

^ Interior of Matchworks Phase II
MORLEY VON STERNBERG

mitigate the clumsiness that is so often apparent where office buildings touch the landscape, a fourth storey (ground floor) is concealed behind a landscaped mound – with only its entrance revealed on the diagonal axis which bisects the water tower of the Matchworks itself. This entrance leads into a formal central space with lift and stair arranged symmetrically, and a steel-tube 'mini atrium' running through all four storeys to a typical Matchworks-style 'chimney' rooflight above. All internal surfaces are finished in basic materials – steel, concrete, glass – enhanced by the use of primary red for tea points and atrium tubes, and yellow for the washroom doors. The building is fully glazed on all four elevations, and employs full-height automatic external blinds for solar control. The decision was made to express the 'floating' structure of the offices in a silver steel frame, the proportions of which pick up on the overall gridiron framed appearance of the original Match Factory.

The 1948 Building

Very different in concept from the 'Matchbox', the 1948-building regeneration still forms a part of Matchworks Phase II, and was built under the same contract. The 1948 building (a post-war addition to the 1918 factory) was constructed to house the match store. It had a heavyweight lower structure with an in situ concrete flat-slab construction, and an upper warehouse behind brick-and-glass façades designed to the overall Match Factory planning grid and glazing proportions. During redevelopment, the subdivision of space to provide flexible commercial/light-industrial units used the well-tried central-core (pod) layout concept with services and washrooms, and a double-beam construction carrying a lightweight roof.

Owing to a two-metre fall in levels across the site, it was necessary to approach the building from both sides, with offices above at the higher half-level and semi-industrial units below amongst the large-diameter in situ concrete mushroom columns. To accommodate the level change, the upper storey is accessed by a boardwalk-style deck running the length of the building, and each entrance point is punctuated by a red steel portal (emblematic of the whole Matchworks development). Again, primary colours are used throughout for significant features – red for steel

portals and yellow for internal 'pods'. These two quite different elements within the Phase II concept are therefore rendered complementary in style, and show how modern new-build can sit comfortably with refurbishment of the old.

Project Evaluation

The Matchworks project as a whole, and particularly Phase II, has been a successful architectural venture, achieved with the help of a flexible, imaginative client. The whole process progressed relatively smoothly, and the projects proved to be a pleasure to work on for all concerned. The only caveat to this appraisal would relate to the longevity of the process – which, by 2009 was into its 13th year! The reasons for this were not really within the architects' remit, including as they did the complexity of the financing, and the developer's programming and long-term intentions.

The works undertaken at Matchworks and the new-build Matchbox illustrate how clusters of commercial units in out-of-town areas need not resemble soulless business parks, devoid of character and quality. The development's location, on the main route from Liverpool John Lennon Airport into the city centre, provides an early glimpse for visitors of the architectural quality that helps define the city.

PROJECT TEAM

Client: **Urban Splash Limited**
Architect: **shedkm architects**
Main Contractor: **Urban Splash BUILD**
Quantity Surveyor: **Simon Fenton Partnership**
Structural Engineer: **Bingham Davis Ltd**
Services Engineer: **Progressive Design Services**
Project Manager: **shedkm with SNOOK**

ST PAUL'S SQUARE

Old Hall Street, Liverpool

Architect: RHWL Architects
Construction Value: £90 million
Completion Date: Phase I: April 2008
Phase II: April 2009
Phase III: February 2011
Project Type: New-build and public realm

Introduction

Liverpool's St Paul's Square was the first of several major development projects for the English Cities Fund (ECf), which aimed to show that high-quality urban regeneration schemes provided viable, attractive and worthwhile opportunities for institutional investors in the medium and long term.

All of ECf's projects are mixed use and are required to demonstrate the quality, scale and critical mass to ensure that they achieve – and maintain – a step-change in the areas concerned.

For years Liverpool has lacked the Grade 'A' office accommodation necessary to compete with new space in Manchester, Newcastle, Leeds and other provincial cities. With no new-build commercial space developed in the prime office core for over ten years, little rental growth and a lack of large floorplates, the city was not seen as an attractive proposition.

The challenge for ECf was to deliver a quality of design and sustainability (both in buildings and the public realm) to surpass any other mixed-use development in the city of Liverpool over the past 20 years or so. The budget available to fund urban mixed-use regeneration was directly related to office rental values, and at the time of the design brief office rents were less than £175 per m².

Client's Brief

The design requirements for St Paul's Square were for an environmentally sound office development. The quality of accommodation was to be the best yet delivered onto the Liverpool commercial market. Flexibility, allowing multi-let occupation, was deemed essential, with highly efficient floorplates within an advanced envelope that would provide the city with

a world-class addition to its architectural heritage and landscape. Fully compliant with all the relevant British Council for Offices (BCO) design standards and guidelines, the office was also to be BREEAM rated 'Very good' or 'Excellent'; BREEAM being the recognised industry standard for benchmarking sustainability.

In a city with such a strong and dynamic heritage of commercial and civic buildings, the client was seeking a group of buildings that could compete with that heritage whilst breaking new ground with respect to sustainability and quality. These challenges were never seen as insurmountable, and the evidence of how they can be met within the constraints previously referred to are now there for all to see.

Design Process

The scheme is the first phase of the intended new commercial district, centred on Old Hall Street and Pall Mall. St Paul's Square will be the gateway from Old Hall Street into the development, which is designed to provide in excess of 140,000 m² of Grade 'A' offices, new high-quality public realm, ancillary leisure and car parking.

Architecture is nothing if not an enterprising and innovative pursuit. The best examples are those that pioneer invention whilst searching for simplicity. When developers venture into the speculative market, they are always faced with the task of exploiting the ingenuity of their design team whilst tempering its exuberance. St Paul's Square should be read as a series of inventive techniques, making the whole greater than the sum of its parts.

The St Paul's Square group of buildings has been developed as a 'family' rather than a collection of different typologies. That is to say, the structures are a collective response to the local context and the wider Liverpool vernacular.

Each member of this family has its own character because of its own immediate context. Each building has drawn upon its position, orientation and neighbours when developing its architectural response, whilst at the same time embracing the common architectural themes of Liverpool. Whether that be in the robust, solid symmetry of the city's major public buildings or the cutting-edge technology of construction and engineering techniques, such as those displayed at Oriel Chambers, St Paul's Square looks to the future whilst recognising the importance of the city's past.

The buildings were also developed using state-of-the-art, modern methods of construction and environmental modelling in order to make them efficient to build and run, and quick to assemble. That has in no way detracted from the quality of the product, its eye for detail and its use of materials – issues already embodied in Liverpool's historic townscape. A surprising and welcome aspect of St Paul's Square is how much people are intrigued by the fact that one architect could design such different buildings. The architects' surprise is how anyone could think they would design any two buildings alike. Their designs, like any family, may share the same DNA but they are all different 'characters'.

The first phase of development was completed in Autumn 2007, and comprises No. 1 St Paul's Square, a 11,700 m² office building which was pre-let to law firm Hill Dickinson LLP and Allied Irish Bank, a 400-space car park and an 11-storey, 50-apartment residential tower – all designed to overlook the square.

No. 5 St Paul's Square represented the second phase of works, and comprises an eight-storey 12,500 m² Grade 'A' office building, which was the only new-build office development to be completed in Liverpool during 2008. With panoramic roof terraces overlooking the city skyline, and a glazed bridge spanning its double-height reception area, No. 5 St Paul's Square is built to the highest standards of design and technology.

Project Evaluation

St Paul's Square is at the heart of Liverpool's commercial renaissance.

Jim Gill, Chief Executive of economic development agency Liverpool Vision.

St Paul's Square is regarded as the most significant new commercial-office-led development to be built in Liverpool city centre within the last decade, and is now – as intended – the focal point for the city's brand new commercial business district.

'St Paul's Square' is now widely regarded as the most sought after and prestigious business address in Liverpool city centre, and No. 5 has already attracted blue-chip tenants such as law firm Davies Wallis Foyster LLP, HBOS (1,100 m² of office space) and Edward Symmons LLP.

∧ Exterior view
HUFTON + CROW

Furthermore, No. 5 St Paul's Square has set very high standards in terms of architecture, design and specification – as well as achieving the city's highest ever rent of £225 per m². The building was sold to Standard Life Investments during construction, an event which marked the first time a fund had invested in an office development in Liverpool for over 20 years – further reinforcing the quality and impact of this particular development.

PROJECT TEAM

Client: **English Cities Fund**
Architect: **RHWL Architects**
Main Contractor: **Shepherd Construction Ltd**
Quantity Surveyor: **Davis Langdon LLP**
Structural Engineer: **Buro Happold**
Services Engineer: **Hannan Associates**
Development Manager: **MUSE Developments**

^ Interior view
PAUL MCMULLIN

Holistically, the building contributed greatly to the transformation of the Ropewalks area.

TEA FACTORY

82 Wood Street, Liverpool

Architect: Urban Splash Architects
Construction Value: £10 million
Completion Date: January 2002
Project Type: Refurbishment

Introduction

The Tea Factory forms part of an area known as the Ropewalks, a commercial and residential district in Liverpool city centre.

In the early 1990s, the area had become run-down and disused. In the mid to late 1990s, however, local developer Urban Splash began improving it – firstly with the redevelopment of Liverpool Palace on Slater Street, followed by the introduction of public space, leisure facilities and apartments at Concert Square and then with the creation of converted office space and apartments at the Tea Factory.

The efforts of Urban Splash over a ten-year period in the area demonstrate the wider context of regeneration and the crucial role that the Tea Factory played in this process. The building attracted niche-market, creative, entrepreneurial organisations, in turn creating employment in the area and bringing new people to the Ropewalks. The Tea Factory is also now home to the Northwest of England branch of the Royal Institute of British Architects (RIBA) as well as the FACT Centre (Foundation for Art and Creative Technology) – bringing cultural audiences, students and a diverse range of people to the area.

Client's Brief

Until the year 2000, the building stood as an empty space. A former tea factory (hence the name!), it was acquired by Urban Splash in 1999 and the company worked closely with architects, surveyors and other specialists to develop designs for the best use of the space. The design team also had to consider the implications for the wider Ropewalks area improvement efforts. The building needed to be somewhere that would attract businesses, create employment and, more importantly, help increase footfall to this part of the

city – which still had a big job to do to convince people that it was a vibrant and fun place to live, work and play.

In addition to the contextual considerations, the development had to be of a high standard of design; retained original features, maximum use of natural light, and definitive commercial and residential layouts all had to be incorporated into the proposals.

The eventual designs saw the creation of more than 5,600 m² of commercial space, with ground-floor retail and leisure space as well as apartments and offices on the upper floors.

Design Process

The Tea Factory was a redundant industrial premises when Urban Splash took on its renovation. The historical development of the site had left a building in two distinct halves: one concrete-framed and an earlier steel-framed construction, both with timber floors. The design developed over time, as is often the case when the client has the benefit of in-house design and construction teams. There were also the kind of opportunities and constraints which redeveloping existing industrial structures inevitably provides.

The Tea Factory building, for example, took up a whole city block, with street frontage to two sides. The opportunity was therefore seized upon to provide a single entry to both these surrounding thoroughfares, as well as a public square fronting St Peter's Church.

At the Tea Factory, it was essential that the four main uses proposed for the building – residential, office, bar and retail – were each given full opportunity to be successful whilst not impacting adversely on one another. The retail and leisure premises would require their own street frontage, whereas the residential and commercial uses would need to have more private,

^ Interior view
PAUL MCMULLIN

^ Exterior view
JOHN STONARD

controlled access. As the building naturally split into two sections by virtue of its hybrid construction methods, the decision was taken to provide a large opening between these halves. It was intended that this would supply the necessary visual 'markers' to denote the residential and commercial uses – and also provide the service, security-control and circulation spaces for these two zones.

The retail and leisure spaces were arranged either side of this entrance slot. The two new floors of apartments were designed to link in with both the existing circulation cores of the former tea factory and also this new slot entrance between the two buildings. The new steel frame connecting to both the historic construction types and structural grids forms a clear, contemporary intervention in the fabric and a light and airy core, as well as having a structural rationale. To top off the building a new roof structure was required to protect the fourth-floor courtyard, from which the apartments would be accessed. An ETFE transparent-foil roof was proposed that would provide the required degree of shelter without compromising necessary ventilation. The apartments proved so popular that they had all sold within a few hours of their release.

Project Evaluation

The Tea Factory project has been a great success, and has become a focus for the design and creative sectors within the Ropewalks area. The building is well used and the gallery spaces and meeting rooms have hosted discussions, debates and exhibitions that have influenced further projects in the city.

Holistically, the building contributed greatly to the transformation of the Ropewalks area. Furthermore, the commitment of organisations such as the RIBA and FACT in moving there instilled great confidence in the wider 'audience' about the appeal of the area. Since the

Tea Factory opened, there have been further developments in the immediate area, encouraged by the success of the scheme and further extending the vibrancy of the area. As such, the project could be described as a catalyst.

The Tea Factory has been almost fully let since Urban Splash completed it at the beginning of 2002. Architects, creative companies and local-authority departments have all worked from there – recent tenants include Liverpool Primary Care Trust, Liverpool Biennial, Places Matter! and MYO Group interior designers.

The residential proposition has also worked well, and all 30 apartments in the building are fully occupied by either owner-occupiers or investor tenants.

PROJECT TEAM

Client: **Urban Splash Limited**
Architect: **Urban Splash Architects**
Main Contractor: **Urban Splash BUILD**
Quantity Surveyor: **Gerrard O'Donnell**
Structural Engineer: **Buro Happold**
Project Manager: **Urban Splash Limited**

111

∧ Interior of Walker Art Gallery
  PAUL MCMULLIN

A PLACE TO VISIT

There are more galleries and museums per
capita in Liverpool than any other place
in the UK, and they are frequented by
Liverpudlians and visitors in their millions.

∨ The Chinese Arch
  PAUL MCMULLIN

∨ American Cruise ship berthed at cruise liner terminal
  PAUL MCMULLIN

∧ Anthony Gormley's 'Another Place'
PAUL MCMULLIN

The Bluecoat gallery, originally a school and Liverpool's oldest surviving building, was at the hub of the city's counter-culture movement in the 1960s. The new Victoria Gallery & Museum was also originally an educational building, and even gave the term 'redbrick' to describe the new wave of metropolitan universities. Its new use continues the theme of adaptation.

Taking a broad definition, 'culture' in Liverpool can include a whole range of activities, from contemporary exhibitions at the Tate to exhibition football at Anfield or Goodison Park. This has long been recognised as a unique selling point for the city, and one of the key themes in its regeneration strategy has been the provision of further cultural activities.

Together, the Tate Gallery, new Museum, new canal link and the Arena have helped to halt the further decline of Liverpool's waterfront, and instead have given new reason to repopulate this area of the city. As a group they are cathartic, reawakening the city not only to major cultural events but also to its singular reason for existence and prosperity — the River Mersey. Whilst the river has

always been the single linking element in the narrative of Liverpool, its association with former good times in the intervening years of economic and social chaos meant that Liverpudlians literally and metaphorically turned their backs on it. What was once seen as a resource became an almost-mocking reference to what had been lost, its constancy and powerful natural force an ironic contrast to the economically enfeebled city in the late 20th century. The early years of the 21st century have shown how this can be reversed.

In contrast to the wide-open spaces of the waterfront, the Ropewalks area of the city is much tighter and more enclosed. Long associated with the worst aspects of the city centre, but always a home for avant-garde Liverpool, this area is now undergoing its own renaissance. Up until the late 1990s the area was seen as peripheral and 'expendable' despite the activities of cultural entrepreneurs such as Urban Splash. Retaining its historic buildings as well as its creative industries, this project has been supplemented both by new buildings and a new media focus. FACT and Toxteth TV beyond the Ropewalks area are both at the forefront of this new activity, with technology and the knowledge economy becoming increasingly important and, driven by a new generation of cultural entrepreneurs, providing new outlets for innovation.

A burgeoning element of this district is its now-thriving nightlife. Since Cream nightclub established itself in the area, Ropewalks has been a focus for independent and alternative enterprises. The once Piranesian appearance of the area, with its romantic overtones of decay, is remembered in the Gothic splendour of the Alma de Cuba bar and restaurant – a former Polish Catholic church, now decidedly rededicated to Bacchus. Nearby, new developments of clubs and bars have been designed with equal zeal but with a Modernist approach. This being Liverpool, the strong geometries and simplicity of these architectural principles have been added to and adapted in order to produce an intelligently crafted group of buildings and public spaces at Concert Steps, which hints at a new Liverpool style of architecture.

> Metropolitan
Cathedral Steps
PAUL MCMULLIN

> Courtyard of
The Bluecoat
PAUL MCMULLIN

> Falkner Street
JOHN STONARD

115

The new Museum of Liverpool is
a landmark tying the attractions
of the riverside and the harbour
to the city.

MUSEUM OF LIVERPOOL

Mann Island, Liverpool

Architect:	3XN, Denmark
Enabling Architect:	AEW
Construction Value:	£72 million
Completion Date:	April 2010
Project Type:	New-build

Introduction

Located within the UNESCO World Heritage Site
between Albert Dock and the Pier Head, and next to a
row of prominent historic buildings dubbed the 'Three
Graces', the new Museum of Liverpool is a landmark
tying the attractions of the riverside and the harbour
to the city. Its structure is conceived as a series of
inclined or elevated platforms, with a central atrium.
The latter serves as a public 'living room' as well as
entrance lobby, providing access to the exhibition
spaces dispersed around it, and a sculptural staircase
acts as the nexus of the building. Interaction of the
public 'promenade' flow with the flow of visitors to the
museum has been key to the design – together with
the provision of a modern, artistic interpretation of the
challenges posed by the site.

The building thus acts as a bridge, both literally and
figuratively. It physically spans the site – the public
'flow' on the Pier Head may pass through its core –
and the exhibitions and collections of the museum will
span Liverpool's past and future. With the ambition
of becoming the world's leading city-history museum,
showcasing social history and popular culture, it is
estimated that the new facility will attract 750,000
visitors a year, thus contributing to the ongoing
regeneration of this former industrial city.

Client's Brief

The historic nature of the site was an important feature
of the brief – as were the client's wishes for the new
museum to act as a symbol of and contributor to the
regeneration of the city, making Liverpool an attractive
tourist destination, and the provision of a place for local
families to find out about their own history.

The brief suggested a more sensitive approach to the
location than previous attempts, so 3XN decided to

^ Exterior of museum facing Albert Dock
PAUL MCMULLIN

treat the museum as a part of the pedestrian flow on the promenade – turning the building, and the area around it, into a meeting place with a structure that would open up the views rather than obstruct them. At the same time, the client wanted a building that would be bold, functional and a social place. This meant that the space should be flexible and dynamic, facilitating changing exhibitions in the galleries. The museum's collection numbers more than 150,000 exhibits, so it was a technical requirement that they be able to be displayed in rotation. Finally, the client wanted a museum in which visitors could start from the centre and choose their own route through the exhibitions. This would obviously provide a certain level of openness, but with a nodal point from where museum-goers could find their own way through the building.

Design Process

Once the client had selected 3XN for the competition, the Danish practice was invited to come to Liverpool and meet with them, to discuss the brief in more detail. This was all in the first week of the design process – after which they had only two weeks to come up with the final design. The whole thing was worked up in the second half of November 2004. Once 3XN had won the competition, the project moved at a very fast pace. The architects began sketching voraciously in the first few weeks, to get a feel for the site and to try and find the best way to approach it. They travelled around the city by vehicle and on foot, talked to people in the street and tried to find out how they would approach the site. Finally, they conceived a dynamic, open and accessible structure that grows out of its riverside site, responding to its context.

Early design models show the struggle of trying to capture the essential aspects of bridging the 'flow' of the site. During the design process the integrated, juxtaposed flow-structures of the atrium, staircases and exhibition-area access were studied thoroughly in sketches, 3D renderings and physical models. The architects made more than 30 models in order to study various possible structures. The museum's panoramic exposure lends itself to 'building in' views of the city and its locations, which are then echoed by every part of the building – gigantic oculi that point to selected historical Liverpool icons.

In addition to its galleries, the museum had to contain a community theatre, space for community exhibitions, auditoriums, learning spaces and a play area for young children. During discussions with the client, it was made clear that they did not want a 'closed box'. With this in mind, 3XN designed the museum so as to enable visitors to walk through it without having to necessarily enter the building itself – even the restaurant is placed 'outside' the building so as to maintain these routes. The project is in fact conceived as 'one big flow' – not just a straightforward building structure – meaning that visitors can move through the museum with ease.

The building is also 'see-through', so that from within one can see outside and vice versa. Framing the views became essential, as did how this 'framing' was perceived externally. Being a city-history museum, it seemed an obvious move to create visual connections between metropolis and museum – making the city itself an exhibit. It was a question of listening to the site and the 'messages' that it was giving to the designers,

∧ Interior of Museum
PAUL MCMULLIN

and finding the story that the building should tell. The 'wings' which shape the main building volume are clad in a whitish natural stone. In the process of making hundreds of sketches, the layout of this stone cladding was found and set in a pattern in which relief, reflections and texture would give the façade a high level of detail.

Project Evaluation

The new Museum of Liverpool is due to open in 2010, which means that it is premature to evaluate the project as a whole. Furthermore, 3XN has not been involved in the construction phase, and thus some details have not been carried out strictly according to their original design. Nonetheless, the architects are keen to know, in the final evaluation of the design, whether they have succeeded in creating the intended strong interaction between city and museum, and whether their solutions to the questions of visitor flow were the right ones.

It already seems as if the sculptural form of the building will become a significant landmark addition to Pier Head and its 'Three Graces' – to the obvious delight of the designers, who are immensely proud of what they have achieved on Liverpool's world-famous waterfront. To mention just one important site-related factor: a key aspect during the early design stages was ensuring planning permission; as a UNESCO World Heritage Site, this issue was extremely sensitive. Thus, looking back, the careful preparations and the strategy leading up to the granting of planning permission by the City Council

as early as in December 2005 was an essential part of ensuring the project's viability.

The Museum of Liverpool has been awarded the IDA Award 2008 for Best Urban Design, and the Bienal Miami + Beach Silver Medal in 2006.

PROJECT TEAM

Client: **National Museums Liverpool**
Architect: **3XN, Denmark**
Enabling Architects: **AEW**
Main Contractor: **E. Pihl & Son A.S, Galliford Try**
Quantity Surveyor: **Turner & Townsend**
Structural Engineer: **Buro Happold**
Services Engineer: **Buro Happold**
Project Manager: **Kim Herforth Nielsen**
Landscape Architect: **Schønherr Landskab**

The architecture of the Arena and Convention Centre responds to its extraordinary waterfront context with a low, sculptural form, making a strong contemporary intervention in the historic setting.

∧ Arena façade at sunset
PAUL MCMULLIN

> PAUL MCMULLIN

ARENA AND CONVENTION CENTRE LIVERPOOL

Monarchs Quay, Liverpool

Architect: Wilkinson Eyre Architects
Construction Value: £146 million
Completion Date: January 2008
Project Type: New-build

Introduction

King's Waterfront, to the southwest of Liverpool's city centre, is a highly sensitive area, created by the infilling of a portion of Liverpool's famous, but now inactive, docks and the clearance of associated buildings. The site, part of the renowned river frontage to the Mersey, is important in both historical and visual terms, being adjacent to the listed (and now regenerated) Albert Dock and near to the 'Three Graces' further to the north. These areas, together with further historic buildings to the east at Wapping Dock, form Liverpool's Maritime Mercantile City World Heritage Site, as designated by UNESCO in 2004.

Wilkinson Eyre's Arena and Convention Centre, which formed the focal point for the city's Capital of Culture celebrations in 2008, occupies approximately 50 per cent of a wider development site on King's Waterfront and comprises a multi-purpose 10,000-seat arena, a conference centre with a 1,350-seat auditorium and a 3,600 m² exhibition hall. There are also two hotels, a 1,600-space multi-storey car park and 100 residential units – all set within and around a major new public open space.

The constraints of this highly sensitive site imposed significant parameters in the development of the design, and extensive pre-planning consultation was carried out with the local authority, English Heritage and other interest groups.

Client's Brief

Owing to its historic setting the brief for this high-profile project called for architecture of the highest quality, with aspirations that the design would serve to augment Liverpool's regenerated waterfront with a landmark structure.

The detailed competition brief identified the various components of the development and sought to place a range of buildings within a previously prepared masterplan for the wider King's Waterfront site. Wilkinson Eyre spearheaded an initiative for an alternative masterplan that grouped the civic facilities together at the northern end of the site.

Further design initiatives driven by Wilkinson Eyre included conjoining the main facilities – the arena and conference centre – in order to enable them to share common elements, and to place the new civic buildings onto the waterfront. The competition masterplan had proposed 'masking' the new buildings' river edge with plots of residential development. However, Wilkinson Eyre was keen to convince the client that the new buildings should be celebrated, and should extend the historic lineage of key landmark buildings along the world-famous Mersey waterfront.

Design Process

Having won the commission, Wilkinson Eyre worked closely with the client body – headed by Liverpool Vision – and their technical representatives in order to establish the brief and develop the initiatives outlined above. The design team worked closely with masterplanners EDAW in order to embody the revised arrangement for the civic facilities into the overall masterplan, for which they were responsible.

The scheme was thus developed and taken to planning-application stage in conjunction with the overall King's Waterfront masterplan. The design teams for both the civic facilities and the masterplan held joint consultations with the client body, local authority and local interest groups up to planning stage. Both aspects of the development were submitted for planning, and presented to the Planning Committee, at the same time.

∧ View from Liverpool One
PAUL MCMULLIN

From the outset, it was clear that the historic setting and aspirations of the client demanded buildings of the highest quality. Whilst many similar facilities elsewhere amount to little more than industrial 'sheds', Wilkinson Eyre was anxious to encourage the client to push for unashamedly contemporary and exciting pieces of architecture that would have a strong visual identity.

Developed with 3D computer technology and using an approach akin to modern product design, the form of the building was developed as a 'virtual' model from an early stage. The lower levels are principally in situ concrete, with a steel-framed 'armature' comprising the sculpted form of the building. This electronic model was provided to the structural-steel and cladding subcontractors, who were able to develop their structural and building-envelope designs directly from it.

The architecture of the Arena and Convention Centre responds to its extraordinary waterfront context with a low, sculptural form, making a strong contemporary intervention in the historic setting. An enhanced public realm reinforces linkages across the site and to the city centre and waterfront beyond, and is enlivened with cultural and artistic activity, retail outlets, cafés and restaurants.

The optimum arrangement for the arena, conference centre and exhibition space is as a single complex, with direct links to supporting facilities such as hotels and car parks. The solution provides two related, sculptural forms on either side of a glazed 'galleria'. The design is inherently flexible, and utilises a horseshoe-shaped configuration for the main seating 'bowl'. A dramatic concourse beneath the exposed underside of the bowl provides an exciting entrance into the new space. The concourse is expressed externally through a glazed circulation zone offering views both in and out to the river and city. The conference centre is conceived as a complementary architectural form to its neighbour, housing the main auditorium, a multi-purpose exhibition hall and a suite of dedicated support spaces.

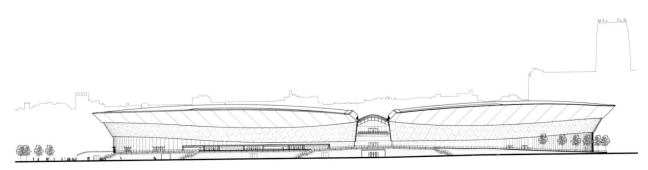

∧ Elevation
SUPPLIED BY WILKINSON EYRE ARCHITECTS

^ Exterior from Albert Dock
PAUL MCMULLIN

^ Atrium Interior
PAUL MCMULLIN

Viewed from the river, the shape of the development contrasts with yet complements the adjacent Albert Dock buildings, and resembles a pair of graceful outstretched arms spanning between Liverpool's famous Anglican and Roman Catholic cathedrals on the skyline beyond. At night, these 'arms' appear to float on a crystalline base, arranged in three sweeping horizontal bands of varied transparency – clear glass at the base, an intermediate layer of patterned translucent glazing and an overhanging aluminium panelled rainscreen.

Project Evaluation

Environmental sustainability, economic growth and improved social cohesion were key drivers for the scheme, and as such the design team embraced them right from the start. The result is a building with impressive sustainability credentials, which is currently the 'greenest' arena and convention centre in Europe. It has achieved a BREEAM environmental rating of 'Very good' – having been designed to emit only half the CO_2 emissions it would have done without any environmentally friendly measures, and to use 20 per cent less electricity than a 'standard' building of its type.

The regeneration of this area of Liverpool has contributed to the success of the surrounding developments such as the Albert Dock and has created a 'draw', bringing people to the waterfront by providing a welcome area for leisure activities.

It has been genuinely adopted, both by the people of Liverpool and by the leisure and conference industries – an outcome clearly demonstrated by the fact that, since opening, the Arena has far exceeded its expectations regarding bookings. It is hoped that it will continue to be successful, and will act as a catalyst to the regeneration of the open dockland further to the south.

The Arena and Convention Centre has received a number of awards, including the following:

- Civic Trust NightVision Special Award 2009
- Civic Trust Award 2009
- RIBA Award 2008
- Regeneration & Renewal Awards 2008: Best Design-Led Regeneration Development (Commendation)
- World Architecture Festival Awards 2008: High Commendation.

PROJECT TEAM

Client: **Liverpool City Council**
Architect: **Wilkinson Eyre Architects**
Main Contractor: **Bovis Lend Lease**
Structural Engineer: **Buro Happold**
Services Engineer: **Faber Maunsell**
Landscape Architect: **Gustafson Porter**
Acoustics: **Sandy Brown Associates**
Lighting Consultant: **Speirs and Major Associates**
Sport Consultant: **Sport Concepts**
Theatre Consultant: **Theatre Projects**

^ Exterior view from University Square
PAUL MCMULLIN

VICTORIA GALLERY & MUSEUM

Ashton Street, Liverpool

Architect: Levitt Bernstein
Construction Value: £6.4 million
Completion Date: May 2008
Project Type: Renovation

Introduction

The Victoria Building was the University of Liverpool's first purpose-built headquarters. Designed in 1889 by the great Liverpool-born Victorian architect Alfred Waterhouse, its landmark clock tower, sited at the crown of Brownlow Hill, rivals the city's two cathedrals for visual impact. Levitt Bernstein's recent project restores and converts the run-down academic building in order to create the Victoria Gallery & Museum. For the first time, this well-known Liverpool landmark has been opened to the general public, to become the university's 'front door' and showcase.

The project's aims have been articulated by Professor Kelvin Everest as:

reaffirming the enduring values of the University's foundation, turned outwards towards the public, and at the centre of our commitment to widening access to the University and participation in its activities and educational provision.

The scheme combines restoration of impressive, highly decorated Grade II listed façades and interiors with judicious modernisation, in order to create state-of-the-art display galleries and to transform an underused asset into an accessible facility at the heart of the university campus.

Client's Brief

The aims of the project, as defined by the university, were to:

- Create a unique visitor attraction for Liverpool and the region;
- Provide an expanded museum and art gallery, with appropriate security and environmental conditions;
- Overcome perceived barriers between the university and the community, and encourage greater involvement by demonstrating the work of the university through activities linked to the displays;
- Lay the foundations for the provision of full access to the university's heritage collections;
- Provide a clear focus point on campus, and a public interface between University and Town;
- Upgrade and refurbish the Leggate Theatre lecture hall.

The converted building contains the university's art and heritage collections, as well as the headquarters of the university's Educational Opportunities Department, administrative offices and a café.

Design Process

The fine building had become run down, and its spaces were unsuitable for modern teaching uses. For its transformation into a successful public building, the status of the entrance was a crucial consideration. The original door was approached by steps from a narrow, crowded pavement along the busy traffic artery of Brownlow Hill.

A key decision was therefore to move the entrance to Ashton Street, the principal pedestrian spine linking major university buildings on both sides of Brownlow Hill. This new entrance was created by lowering windows to ground level and raising the floor of the new reception area to provide a level route from the outside through to Waterhouse's spectacular double-height hall. From this point, the eye is drawn to the first-floor galleries, which are accessed by the original grand stair and a new lift.

A second crucial choice was the location of the new passenger lift in the tower. As a glazed, well-lit and unashamedly modern intervention, it draws attention to the delights on offer on the upper levels and forms

The transformation of an underused and ailing building of great architectural quality has been achieved by subtle interventions, revealing the quality of Waterhouse's interiors to the wider public for the first time.

an enjoyable experience as the visitor travels between floors – with views out to the street, and inward to the hall and stair.

A third major decision concerned the position of the service lift – essential to provide access for large artworks and artefacts to the gallery spaces. It was positioned externally, tucked into a return in the corner of the quadrangle, and clad in metal shingles of varied pattern. Patinated copper was chosen in order to recede visually from the brighter red brick of the original walls, and the shape was selected to emphasise the new tower's slim verticality.

Waterhouse's main set-piece spaces have been restored and re-lit, with subtle interventions to improve their functionality. The great hall and staircase have added sound absorption to lessen sound reflections caused by the hard, tiled surfaces. The Leggate Theatre is a classic semicircular, steeply raked auditorium. It has been sealed from extraneous noise, with curtains and sound-absorbing panels added in order to moderate its reverberation and improve its suitability for speech and chamber music. The natural light which originally flooded through the ceiling has been recreated by means of a light box, now capable of blackout. The magnificent Tate Hall, originally the university's library, has been restored and improved with a light touch, reusing light fittings and adding uplighting in order to highlight the lofty timber-beamed roof. It incorporates restored showcases designed by Waterhouse and retrieved from Manchester Museum.

The more utilitarian teaching spaces are converted to provide art galleries and offices. Dropped ceilings incorporate ventilation and lighting, and maintain the rooms' spacious proportions. Strict environmental controls are possible in the picture galleries, and plant is carefully and unobtrusively installed.

The university's art collections are exhibited on the first floor, and the heritage collections are displayed in the Tate Hall. The Leggate Theatre is now suitable for a variety of uses, including formal university meetings, lectures and music performances. There is a café on the ground floor, located within the stunning double-height hall. The Educational Opportunities Department occupies the ground-floor offices.

Project Evaluation

The Victoria Gallery & Museum is an important addition to Liverpool's attractions. The number of members of the public visiting the university's collections has been vastly increased as a result of the greater prominence, better access and augmented display space provided by their new home. The transformation of an underused and ailing building of great architectural quality has been achieved by subtle interventions, revealing the quality of Waterhouse's interiors to the wider public for the first time. The large and ornately designed building has been converted for a relatively small budget, which has required careful consideration of priorities. New features, such as the café and the passenger lift, have been designed in a contemporary style, and sit alongside careful restoration – revealing the essence of Waterhouse's architecture through the medium of an entirely new and appropriate function.

^^ Interior of the café
MORLEY VON STERNBERG

^ Interior staircase
MORLEY VON STERNBERG

Taken together the interventions transform a dowdy, underused and old-fashioned building into a series of elegant and enjoyable public spaces. The beauty of Waterhouse's set-piece interiors may now be appreciated in a fully accessible environment, and the university's fascinating collections are displayed in spaces that finally do justice to their breadth and quality.

PROJECT TEAM

Client: **University of Liverpool**
Architect: **Levitt Bernstein**
Main Contractor: **Kier North West**
Quantity Surveyor: **EC Harris**
Structural Engineer: **Arup**
Services Engineer: **National Design Consultancy**
Project Manager: **University of Liverpool Facilities**
Lighting Consultant: **Light + Design Associates Ltd**
Signage Consultant: **Aukett Brockliss Guy Ltd**

> Concert Steps has been a great success. It has become a focus for this part of the Ropewalks area and a major venue for Liverpool's evening economy.

CONCERT STEPS

Seel Street/Fleet Street/Concert Street, Liverpool

Architect: shedkm architects
Construction Value: £15 million
Completion Date: Ongoing
Project Type: Renovation New Build

∧ Exterior view
PAUL MCMULLIN

∧ Exterior view
PAUL MCMULLIN

Introduction

Concert Steps is the name given to a five-phase development which forms a new square in the heart of Liverpool city centre's Ropewalks district. The design by shedkm architects, with developers Frenson and project managers Chartwell, is the result of a ten-year masterplan process, which uses the remnants of a vacant pre-war city block to inform new minimalist additions that contribute to repairing and enhancing the area's existing built fabric.

Driven by the demand for nightlife entertainment, Concert Steps has been developed as a series of bars, restaurants and clubs, each one varying in size and complexity and each contributing to the evolution of the square.

The vision of the masterplan was to incorporate a series of public spaces which create links between Concert Square and the new developments in and around the Bluecoat.

Through the careful demolition of redundant structures, together with the retention of existing industrial buildings and addition of new-build interventions, the masterplan reinforces the framework of the area whilst increasing its visual and physical permeability, connecting and re-establishing its presence within the city.

Client's Brief

shedkm's involvement with Frenson began in 2000, following the creation of a new square on Concert Street in what became the first of a series of initiatives to encourage movement across the Ropewalks area between Bold Street, Fleet Street and Seel Street.

Frenson facilitated the implementation of this new square by transferring its ownership of a pre-war derelict clothing factory, which was demolished to create space for what is now Concert Square.

The success of the subsequent development highlighted a Frenson-owned warehouse called 26 Fleet Street, which, through the demolitions, had become part of the square's perimeter frontage. At this point, Frenson employed shedkm to design a new-build extension to the building. This became phase one: Walkabout, and through its success it triggered a second phase, Mood, which acted as a key mechanism in unlocking the derelict city block behind.

The brief for the development thus ran in tandem with the masterplan's evolution, reacting to the needs and requirements of interested tenants.

Following the completion of the two phases, Frenson, along with shedkm, began the design of a masterplan informed by the existing city block connected to the completed phases – which itself would become a new square surrounded by bar/restaurant use, creating a new city-centre hub to be called Concert Steps.

Design Process

The five-phase masterplan was initiated with the conversion of a former sailmaker's workshop fronting Concert Square. Currently occupied by 'Walkabout Inns', this first phase provided the opportunity to create a new pedestrian link into Concert Steps through the introduction of a glass, steel and timber-clad extension with an open-air seating terrace.

The success of this initial phase unlocked the development of phase two, which involved the renovation of an 18th-century cabinet manufacturer's warehouse – now operated by 'Mood'. Completed in 2004, this phase involved the demolition of a redundant building behind the warehouse and the installation of a cedar-clad extension. Clearly expressed as a modern addition, the extension provides efficient vertical circulation to all floors of the building, whilst maintaining undisrupted open floorplates within the existing warehouse. Through its location at the rear of the building, this new intervention further facilitates the masterplan through provision of a fully glazed south-facing aspect, which fronts a new central square.

This square, marked by a matured German-imported oak, becomes the 'hub' of the development, and sits at the heart of the masterplan area.

The position and form of the first phases of the masterplan were used as mechanisms to encourage pedestrian movement from the periphery into the centre of the new square, and, through the mediating effect of the existing buildings, level access across the entire site is provided.

Phase three, completed in May 2008, features a new-build, elevated, two-storey cube, which complements the masterplan strategy by contributing the definition of the main square. This cube acts as a mediator, balancing the change in scale between the smaller Seel Street warehouses and the larger factories surrounding the neighbouring Concert Square. Pedestrian access from Seel Street is encouraged by the insertion of a new concrete 'drum' and the introduction of a new-build extension to an existing warehouse as part of phase four.

Phase four completes the perimeter to the main square and defines two new pedestrian routes – one providing access to Fleet Street and the other into a secondary, lower square. The development of phase four retains and restores the existing Seel Street sandstone elevation and introduces a respectfully proportioned new-build extension set back from its elevation by a

glazed atrium. The sandstone façade acts as a new, active frontage to Seel Street, and provides a visual link between the main inner square and the city beyond.

Phase five of the masterplan, currently under design, will complete the development and create a new upper square and further pedestrian links from Fleet Street.

The approach to the masterplan respects and builds upon the industrial heritage of the Ropewalks area. The robust character, form and proportions of the existing buildings are echoed through the use of steel, timber and glass, which not only complement the adjacent buildings but enhance the existing fabric.

Project Evaluation

Concert Steps has been a great success. It has become a focus for this part of the Ropewalks area and a major venue for Liverpool's evening economy. The later stages have enhanced the connections through the area – allowing greater access and an increase in popularity – attracting workers and students alike. It has also become an important addition to the cultural attractions offered by the city to national and international visitors – a true Liverpool experience!

Regeneration winner at the Regional Property Awards in 2005, the masterplan has succeeded in reactivating the redundant city-centre block, whilst encouraging further redevelopment along Seel Street and its periphery.

The phased approach to the masterplan has allowed Frenson to respond to the needs of their tenants whilst enabling the architecture to gradually mature, reflecting the fabric of the existing warehouses and allowing shedkm to design appropriate and informed interventions. As individual insertions, the new-build elements have brought fresh life to a previously redundant city block, and as a collective they create a new hive of activity within Liverpool's Ropewalks district.

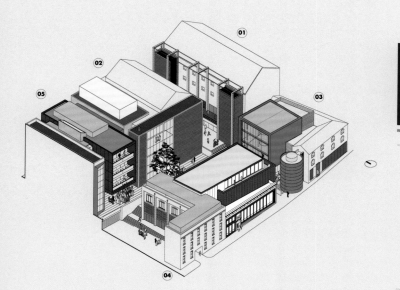

^ Five phases of development, Concert Steps
COURTESY OF SHEDKM ARCHITECTS

PROJECT TEAM

Client: **Frenson Ltd**
Architect: **shedkm architects**
Main Contractor: **Livesey Group, David Mclean Contractors Ltd**
Structural Engineer: **Muir Associates, Sleater & Watson LLP**
Project Manager: **Chartwell Project Management Ltd**
Landscape Architect: **BCA Landscape**

This flagship building is a community-based media centre providing hands-on film, TV and video-production training, and is also home to a cluster of small film-production and creative companies.

∧ Exterior view
PAUL MCMULLIN

TOXTETH TV

38–45 Windsor Street, Liverpool

Architect:	Union North
Construction Value:	£840,000
Completion Date:	June 2003
Project Type:	New-build and reuse

Introduction

Toxteth TV comprises a set of buildings along Windsor Street, which collectively form a 'campus'. It offers new opportunities and ways of learning to help the community in which it is based: firstly, those young people in danger of exclusion from school (a significant cause and effect of the multiple deprivations endured in the area); secondly, people wishing to set up their own enterprises – social or commercial. The community has been decanted, recanted, de-recanted and finally re-recanted, but remains extremely strong, mutually supportive and wonderfully Liverpool 8 – 'The World in One Postcode'.

This flagship building is a community-based media centre providing hands-on film, TV and video-production training, and is also home to a cluster of small film-production and creative companies. With a fixed budget – funded through the Department for Education and Skills (DfES, now the Department for Children, Schools and Families); and European sources – which would usually generate the most rudimentary commercial-park shed, the challenge was to create a response as distinctive as it was economical.

Out of necessity, Toxteth TV was built on a shoestring within a very short and inflexible construction period. Locally sourced labour, materials and minimum energy usage were key drivers for the scheme. Raw, low-cost and reclaimed materials were used in lateral ways in order to create an animated triptych in brick, timber and block – and the buildings were delivered for £600 per m².

Client's Brief

In May 2001, the Toxteth TV team assembled ten individuals with the capital to purchase the Windsor Castle, a former pub, whilst they awaited a funding decision. The place was boarded up and burnt out after standing derelict for over three years, and was adjacent to a council-owned car park – a popular dumping-point for stolen vehicles on the former site of two tower blocks that had been demolished in the mid-1980s. In February 2002, the DfES confirmed funding for the project, and Toxteth TV bought the pub back from its guardians. After protracted negotiations, the team also purchased the adjoining car park from the council, and the design phase began in earnest.

The challenge was to provide a unique building that local residents would be proud of, whilst delivering the required amount of floor area on a shoestring. The building needed to be the catalyst for regeneration in a maligned area. The team commissioned a young, radical firm of architects who had an environmental agenda – Liverpool-based Union North. 'When I think back to the original design brief, I think we wanted a big red box; something visible from a long distance away, which of course would never have got past the planners', recalls Toxteth TV board director, and project purse-strings holder, Nick Stanley. 'The brief evolved in those early stages, but at all times our collective vision was to create something different and special, something that would appeal to a young audience without alienating or offending the wider community and, importantly, something that was environmentally friendly.'

Design Process

There was great debate about whether to retain the pub; the conventional view was that it should be demolished. However, it was a sound, mid-1950s structure and, moreover, the team felt that the environmental impact of consigning a perfectly good construction to a landfill site would have been dishonourable. Instead, the fire-damaged roof was lifted off, and the L-shaped form extended to provide the first of three distinct rectilinear components that contain different building functions.

After widespread community and public consultation, these simple blocks were developed using established construction techniques and familiar, low-cost materials animated by pattern, texture, composition and juxtaposition.

The design team's approach to construction technology and materials was driven largely by cost and time restraints. They had identified from the outset that in order to deliver the project on time and on budget, they would have to steer clear of specialist technologies, complicated detailing and refined materials. Instead, they made use of simple forms and technologies normally employed by volume housebuilders, the aim being to use cheap and readily available materials in an inspired, 'lateral-thinking' manner. Initial investigations explored the use of modified 'off-the-shelf' agricultural barns and modular prefabricated buildings, but these were disregarded partly because they did not meet the security and acoustic-performance criteria required, and also because there were planning concerns regarding the residential context.

The new structures utilised standard loadbearing cavity construction, and floors were constructed from either pre-cast hollow-rib concrete planks or steel with timber joists. Masonry was a logical choice because of its inherent acoustic properties. In the case of the studio, where acoustic performance was critical, the thick inside skin was constructed using dense concrete block (made in Liverpool), laid flat. As much as possible was salvaged from the pub – including the original toilet cubicles and gents' urinals, which were cleaned up and reinstalled. This dogged commitment to retain and reuse saved the developers thousands in sanitaryware alone – releasing budget for more value-adding uses. The TV studio itself is 150 per cent of its originally intended size, because money was saved elsewhere and the costs of extending it were minimal.

In order to minimise construction costs, and reduce waste material, much of the pub's primary structural elements (cavity masonry-wall construction, concrete beam-and-block floors) were retained. Money was so tight that existing window openings were kept where possible. Workspaces were located within the reworked existing building owing to its cellular nature, and these provide the revenue for sustaining the training facilities and recording studio contained in the other two volumes.

The training block sits adjacent to the existing building, hard against the pavement edge, and forms part of the main street elevation. The studio is a large, double-height clear-span space tucked behind the training block, which contains teaching spaces and multimedia rooms. The linking element between the blocks provides communal spaces, and serves as the building's main entrance. Within this central space all materials used externally are drawn together, providing a sense of legibility.

The orientation of the building and the use of space inside and around it are considered, environmentally sensitive and imaginative. A tree on the former car-park site was preserved and incorporated into the design – now pride of place in the centre of a rear courtyard that is used as a break-out space.

Project Evaluation

Despite the design challenges and limitations, the result is a great building for an astonishingly low cost. By using economical, raw and reclaimed materials in unusual and creative ways, the results are both sustainable and striking. These include:

- Reclaimed timber cladding: The retained original brickwork structure was clad with reclaimed timber roof joists, split down their length and wire-brushed on the face. Texture and some colour thus give the façade an entirely new appearance.

- Striped brickwork to training block: 15 different brick types were chosen, and the elevation composed using overlapping stripes of colour. Because of the nature of the composition, the accuracy of the pattern was not critical; however, the result is a stunningly colourful composition.

- Blockwork walls: The external facing block is given texture and pattern by using headers of random blocks, protruding 25 mm from the wall face.

- Marine plywood: The exterior of the main entrance area uses sheets of marine plywood, fitted by yacht builders. This material is very low-cost and exceptionally weatherproof, yet seldom used for building exteriors.

- Sterling-board interior walls: The easily dismantled partitions between office spaces have been clad in sheets of sterling board. The irregular pattern of flattened, softwood strands makes for a raw appearance in tune with the utilitarian feel of the centre.

∧ Exterior view
PAUL MCMULLIN

PROJECT TEAM

Client: **Toxteth TV**
Architect: **Union North**
Main Contractor: **Nobles Construction Ltd**
Quantity Surveyor: **Simon Fenton Partnership**
Structural Engineer: **Buro Happold**
Services Engineer (pre tender): **Fulcrum Consulting**
Services Engineer (post tender): **Steven Hunt Associates**
Acoustic Engineer: **Hepworth Acoustics**

> Latin America was cited as a key inspiration – a region that has also been shaped by an unlikely combination of these same two sources: religion and celebration.

^ Interior
PAUL MCMULLIN

ALMA DE CUBA

Seel Street, Liverpool

Architect:	R2 Architecture and DK Architects
Construction Value:	£650,000
Completion Date:	August 2005
Project Type:	Refurbishment and renovation

Introduction

St Peter's Church in Seel Street is one of the oldest buildings in the city centre. It was erected in 1788, in what was then an almost rural location on the edge of Liverpool. The church survived as a Catholic place of worship until 1976, after which it served the local Polish community for a short time.

A number of scenarios had been proposed for the building, such as offices, which would have seriously damaged the overall aspect of the main space. The client had a history of opening licensed retail premises in listed buildings and decided to convert the building into a bar and restaurant.

The scheme is an important component of the successful regeneration of the Ropewalks area, and forms part of a group of refurbished historic buildings in the area, along with FACT and the Tea Factory, as well as relating to new public space at St Peters Square and Arthouse Square.

Client's Brief

In practical terms, the brief required the creation of a bar on the ground floor of the premises and restaurant with ancillary spaces at the first-floor level. However, at the heart of the project lay a distinctive vision – this was to retain the majestic qualities of what was still in essence a sacred space – and to juxtapose these with the flamboyant spirit and dynamism of the surrounding, re-energised city.

Latin America was cited as a key inspiration – a region that has also been shaped by an unlikely combination of these same two sources: religion and celebration.

Design Process

The main challenge that R2 Architecture and DK Architects faced lay in the fact that the building and its existing internal elements had an inherent strength and history. It was felt essential that any interventions into the existing structure should be as strong as the elements already there. This was achieved through the clear articulation of the interventions made, using a restricted palette of materials and a rigorous simplicity of detailing. The main space has been left relatively intact, with a timber and marble-clad mezzanine inserted in order to provide space for the upstairs restaurant and VIP areas. This mezzanine 'clings' to the existing walls along each side of the old nave of the church – leaving a clear void over the main bar, except for a dramatic, glass-railed bridge. The mezzanine replaces an original gallery, and the original stone access stairs have been retained. However, the gallery, unsafe due to rot, has been replaced by a light-weight structure that allows for 'people-watching' and full views of the main ground floor space.

The stunning downstairs bar is also clad entirely in the same Indian marble, while its floor surface is a textured, cracked stone. All these simple, but beautifully detailed, elements serve to highlight and focus attention on the altar, which has been partially restored, dramatically lit and which now plays a large role in the success of the overall scheme.

That said, the interventions that were made display a level of clarity that enables them to act as counterpoints to the existing elements. It was essential that they had a sense of integrity and form, and would not just be subordinate to the main, existing features. One of the major generators for the scheme, for example, was the decision to deny the space the symmetry that was implied by its ecclesiastical history. The bar was positioned off-centre within the full-height opening created by the U-shaped first-floor plan.

Alma de Cuba also contains some other hidden

^ Interior view
PAUL MCMULLIN

∨ Interior view
PAUL MCMULLIN

surprises – from the club-room feel of the old Lady Chapel to the suspended wall-to-wall-to-ceiling wallpapered 'box' of the upstairs bar (like an inside-out Christmas present) and the external terrace. This terrace is linked to the inside spaces by the boldly placed, double-height, structurally glazed opening that also provides a visual link to the semi-private space of the upstairs bar.

Project Evaluation

The main problems for the venue have, thankfully, been its great success. The ground-floor bar soon required an additional satellite service bar in order to cope with the number of patrons requiring service. Additionally, it was discovered that temperatures can rise beyond the comfortable level at busy times – and this was rectified by the introduction of openable skylights, which had been proposed in the initial scheme.

Liverpool has always been a cosmopolitan and global city, largely due to its maritime and commercial history. Whilst over the last four decades the lack of investment in the city has not always matched its previously global status and aspirations, Liverpool is now once again a destination for urban explorers, both national and international. Unique projects such as the Alma de Cuba demonstrate that the city's tradition of inventiveness and irreverence still remains as part of its contemporary character.

PROJECT TEAM

Client: **Robert Gutmann**
Architect: **R2 Architecture and DK Architects**
Main Contractor: **Bridgewater Contracts**
Structural Engineer: **Booth King Partnership Limited**
Services Engineer: **Bridgewater contractor design**
Project Manager: **Johnny Holt**

> Interior view
showing the en-
trance and staircase
PAUL MCMULLIN

The popular appeal of films provides FACT with the opportunity to mix entertainment and appreciation of the arts, in the context of a social hub.

FACT CENTRE

88 Wood Street, Liverpool

Architect:	Austin-Smith:Lord LLP
Construction Value:	£10 million
Completion Date:	2003
Project Type:	New-build

Introduction

The FACT Centre (Foundation for Art and Creative Technology) is an arts project for the digital age – incorporating art galleries and space for on-line and streaming broadcast material, combined with three commercial cinema screens.

FACT has its roots in voluntary arts activity which emanated from the Bluecoat Arts Centre, another city-centre arts consortium. Its aim is to support 'artists' work and innovation in the fields of film, video and new media'.

Hampered by inadequate accommodation at the Bluecoat, FACT – led by its first director, Eddie Berg, who subsequently became a director at the National Film Theatre – won Lottery funding for a new complex in the historic regeneration area of Ropewalks.

Crucial to the sustainability of the centre has been the management's pragmatic commitment to intellectual as well as physical accessibility.

A partnership with City Screen, the commercial art-house cinema group, and a policy of celebrating good work rather than exclusively avant-garde films has ensured FACT vast popular support for excellence and has introduced multitudes to the progressive arts. Critical finance has brought security, programming and distribution access.

FACT opened in 2003, and has developed to become a popular venue where people of all ages gather to socialise, watch films and enjoy art.

Client's Brief

The founding director of FACT envisioned an arts centre relevant to everyday life, which would nonetheless provide all the facilities needed for the development of art forms at the cutting edge of digital technology.

From the point of view of its social context, the building was required to combine commercial cinema auditoriums with gallery space, and to provide accommodation for artists in residence, with hands-on facilities for the general public, plus offices for the organisation's administration team.

The popular appeal of films provides FACT with the opportunity to mix entertainment and appreciation of the arts, in the context of a social hub.

The inclusive and social nature of film-going generates the need for foyers which are more than crush spaces. Bars, cafés and retail outlets which are convenient to the exhibition spaces and to the 'screens' were also required.

The limited site – in a critical, central location – imposed a complex spatial assembly, which nevertheless needed to process large numbers of visitors in a logical and resource-efficient manner. All FACT's facilities needed to be easily accessible and easy to find. The spatial assembly had to reflect the hierarchy of functional requirements and needed to present the key components of the FACT with equal emphasis. It needed to be a legible and accessible network of activity and facility.

The whole complex was also envisaged as a regenerative catalyst for the Ropewalks area and adjacent Bold Street, one of the original shopping gateways to Liverpool city centre. It was to host fledgling and complementary arts organisations, yet also attract secular gatherings as part of the wider conferencing 'offer' for Liverpool city centre.

Design Process

FACT's concept of mixing creative digital technology, as an art form, with architecture is the result of a creative collaboration between the architects and an artist in residence (Clive Gilman), with the facilitation of a visionary client.

The artist's involvement added a questioning, whimsical component to the usually intense briefing and planning process. The outcome is a building management system which animates sound systems and LED arrays integrated into the main elevations. The elevations themselves, with their deep-drawn titanium-zinc cladding trays and picture window, are symbolic of the pixelation seen on TV screens, whilst the LEDs are representative of the latest colour-TV test screen. The rear elevation integrates two massive projection screens, for open-air viewing of film from a public square which has been created on the adjacent site.

FACT's four-storey foyer (or 'street') puts its entire 'offer' on show. In the context of a restrained colour palette, construction materiality is expressed as a contextual and functional response to the grittiness of the area and its culture. The monochrome, exposed, fairfaced concrete walls; black, polished concrete floor; and cantilevered in situ staircase are all offset by the russet hue of the Corten self-oxidizing steel used as a decorative overcladding to the box office.

The main 'black box' gallery volume is complemented by two other spaces: an informal area, formed by the undercroft of one of the cinemas, which has proved immensely popular with artists; and 'the Box', a hybrid gallery-cum-function-space immediately off the entrance 'street'. The Box doubles as a media lounge in which the audience can enjoy films from the comfort of sofas, which can be stored under the gallery floor when the space is used for exhibitions or indeed for receptions.

The centre's cinemas, which show artistically acclaimed mainstream films alongside art-house productions, have been designed to full THX (high-fidelity sound reproduction) standards, and have reclining seats. The quality and accessibility of these auditoriums in central Liverpool has made them appealing to the wider business community, so that during the daytime (when films are not traditionally shown) the centre has hosted significant conferences.

The cinemas are all housed at first-floor level, accessed from entrance level by a processional, cascade staircase. The treads each cantilever 2.5 m from an in situ concrete wall. The importance of the cinemas is further acknowledged by partially cantilevering the 'screens' over the street – with the pendulous, curved underbellies of the raked seating floating like stylised clouds.

Behind FACT, a commercial development, the Arthouse (also by Austin-Smith:Lord), has incorporated a public space between the two buildings. The cinema spaces within FACT are externally expressed as projecting boxes and the 'reverse' of the screens is actually developed as an external projection surface facing the square. Powerful projectors housed in the Arthouse development show films on these external screens, to audiences partying in Arthouse Square.

Key to the success of FACT is its mix of shop, café and bar – all open and accessible to passers-by at all times. They are all located on the 'internal street' which links Wood Street and Arthouse Square, through the building. The assembly of functions and spaces has generated a lively, active venue where people-watching and promenading coexist with conferencing, in addition to the visiting of exhibitions and the watching of films.

The more private offices and artists spaces sit on the roof of the whole complex. Given the deep footprint of the lower parts of the building, this allows natural daylight and ventilation to all rooms, as well as providing spectacular views over the rooftops of the city centre towards the River Mersey.

Project Evaluation

An overwhelming success since it opened, the Foundation for Art and Creative Technology has become an arts-focused gathering place for the wider city community. Young people and seniors mingle there every night, and earnest arts types hang out by day alongside business groups which use the auditoriums for conferencing in between the film shows.

Liverpool hosts the Biennial Art Festival for the visual arts and as one of the city's 'Big Five' arts organisations, the FACT Centre has played a leading role in collaborating, curating and hosting these successful, city-wide events. FACT's location has opened up the city to new audiences with challenging, progressive work as well as to the enjoyment of good films.

The building has proved to be eminently adaptable. Shortly after opening, a serious failure of the suspended ceiling in one of the cinemas resulted in a protracted closure of some of the centre's facilities but was swiftly overcome by the adaptation of 'the Box' for film shows. Since reopening, FACT's popularity has continued undiminished.

The current director, Mike Stubbs, has pressed the building to accommodate even more shows, by 'rigging' the street in order to fly exhibition pieces, like the animatronics of Bernie Lubell. Similarly, he is making the bar areas double as venues for participative events. Here, Jean Grant's Settlement crossed borders between environmental art and planning, attracting thousands of participants and opening a new debate about creativity in the normally bureaucratic process of town planning.

Sitting in an area of regenerative opportunity, FACT has had significant influence outside its immediate locale but is now generally considered to have reached saturation in terms of its usability. Plans are afoot for expansion into neighbouring properties, which will build on FACT's founding design principles of inclusive legibility and urbanity.

> Exterior view
PAUL MCMULLIN

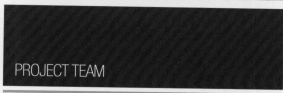

PROJECT TEAM

Client: **FACT**
Architect: **Austin-Smith:Lord LLP**
Main Contractor: **Mowlem**
Quantity Surveyor: **Rex Proctor & Partners**
Structural Engineer: **Buro Happold**
Services Engineer: **Buro Happold**
Project Manager: **Gardiner & Theobald Management Services**

∨ The FACT Centre, cross section
AUSTIN-SMITH:LORD LLP

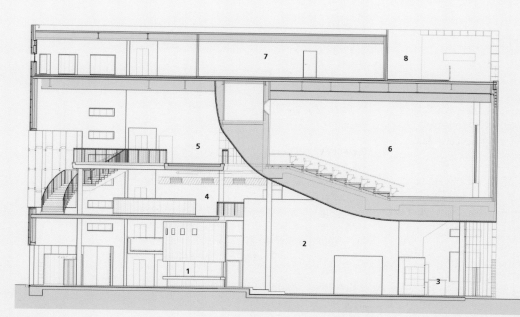

1. Tickets and Information
2. The Box
3. Cafe
4. Bar
5. Kiosk
6. Screen 2
7. FACT HQ
8. Roof Terrace

The opening of the Tate
Liverpool in 1988 really marked
the successful completion of the
Albert Dock restoration and the
beginning of the first phase of
Liverpool's rehabilitation from its
pariah status.

^ interior view showing entrance space
PAUL MCMULLIN

TATE LIVERPOOL

Albert Dock, Liverpool

Architect: James Stirling/Michael Wilford Associates
Construction Value: Not known
Completion date: May 1988
Project Type: Refurbishment

Introduction

The Tate Gallery is located at Albert Dock on Liverpool's
waterfront. Designed by the Dock Engineer, Jesse
Hartley, and opened in 1845, the warehouse pavilions
at Albert Dock are all listed Grade I, and are widely
recognised as the largest such group in the country.
Renowned architectural historian Nikolaus Pevsner
thought Albert Dock 'one of the finest examples
anywhere in Europe of romantic architecture parlante',
i.e. of expressing the strength of resistance to water
and the bulk of ships. Writing in the late 1960s, when
the Dock was redundant and falling into decay, Pevsner
added that it would be a 'black disgrace' if the group
were to be demolished. It is scarcely credible now, but
this was almost its fate, with several proposals over a
period of two decades designed around total or partial
demolition – or even infilling the central water space as
a car park!

Fortunately for Albert Dock, a combination of the city's
near-bankruptcy and political upheaval ensured that
the buildings, and the dock, remained, although in a
perilous state. The public outcry that found a voice in
Quentin Hughes's eloquent book *Seaport* grew following
the 1981 Toxteth riots, when Liverpool's reputation as
a problem city was sealed by national and international
headlines exposing the city's failure to rise to the
challenge of economic and social meltdown.

Client's Brief

Despite the political enmity then existing between the
national Conservative administration and Liverpool's
Labour ruling group, Mrs Thatcher's Secretary of State
for the Environment, Michael Heseltine, became the
'Minister for Merseyside', and a new strategy was
established based on the creation of the Merseyside
Development Corporation (MDC), the first of a new
generation of regeneration companies within the UK

responsible for tackling some of the worst-performing
urban areas. Acting as a focus for investment, and with
a remit that included the poor physical infrastructure
of the waterfront and specifically the south docks, the
MDC quickly pulled together a strategy that featured
the restoration of Albert Dock as one of its main
objectives. Intended to be 'pump-primed' by the public
sector, London-based company Arrowcroft was quick to
recognise its potential and provided the private-sector
investment required.

In 1981, the Tate Gallery had already decided to
open a northern facility, and Liverpool's high national
profile secured the city as its chosen destination.
James Stirling was already working for the Tate on
their London gallery, and he was asked to undertake
the new Liverpool venue. The choice was inspired:
Stirling, although born in Scotland, was a graduate of
the Liverpool School of Architecture. He had already
worked within Merseyside, but his buildings were often
controversial and he refused to be pinned down by
reference to any particular style.

Design Process

Stirling's work for the Tate at Albert Dock was
commissioned at a juncture in the architect's working
life at which he was moving from a personal approach
to Modernism to a reinvention of that style's precepts
which was later to be named 'Postmodernism' (although
this was a tag he himself consistently rejected). In
Liverpool, Stirling's conversion of Hartley's dockside
structures is an exemplar of simplicity and clarity that
allows the building and its function to speak for itself.
This is far removed from the architect's flamboyant
approach to other projects, and his interventions at the
Tate speak more of deference and respect to Hartley
than a wish on Stirling's part to trump the original
designer.

The Albert Dock stacks are each of five storeys, constructed with a brick skin on a cast-iron frame – the whole standing on beech piles. A colonnade – supported on oversized Doric, cast-iron columns – runs around the whole of the dock, allowing waterside access to the ground floors of the warehouses. Hartley's elevations are simply articulated, with arched windows and vertical hoisting slots that provide a regular rhythm, and an unfussy modulation to the façades.

Internally, Stirling essentially carried out minimal intervention in the form of a refit, adapting the existing building to its new purpose. A mezzanine was provided within the existing structural frame, in which each floor was supported by a system of cast-iron columns and beams and simple arched vaults. The stressed-skin roof was made of wrought-iron plates riveted together and tied by wrought-iron rods, so that its strength was derived from the curved skin itself, and not from roof trusses. The whole, elegant ensemble was fireproof.

Within this shell, Stirling used the existing spine wall for the new stair and lift core. On either side of this, galleries were laid out that simply slotted into the space created by Hartley. Some of the servicing is hidden behind the new walls necessary to hang artwork, but most of the servicing and lighting is contained in visible ducts hanging beneath the ceiling arches. Stirling's foyer design included a café and bookshop at mezzanine level, overlooking the entrance. In the architect's original scheme, the entrance to the new Tate was marked by a panelled blue-and-orange colour scheme punched with portholes and simple signage, although much of this has been subsequently replaced by glazing.

Project Evaluation

The opening of the Tate Liverpool in 1988 was a crucial milestone in the successful completion of the Albert Dock restoration and the beginning of the first phase of Liverpool's rehabilitation from its pariah status. It is entirely appropriate that this landmark was achieved by James Stirling, an adopted son of the city with an international profile and importance.

The success of the Tate and the Albert Dock was the first sign that Liverpool's much-troubled recent past could be healed through physical intervention in its fabric, and an approach to regeneration that relied in part on acknowledging its maritime history. The first few years of the reinvented Albert Dock attracted five million visitors per annum to the city, and, just as importantly, became a good news story locally, nationally and internationally following years of negative publicity. The Tate has become a cornerstone of Liverpool's cultural 'offer' and a major tourist destination in its own right. Stirling's departure from his recognised approach to design in other projects is what stands out in the Tate scheme, and his genius rests in allowing the building to retain its industrial majesty and power.

^^ Interior view of gallery space
PAUL MCMULLIN

^ Basement cloakroom area
PAUL MCMULLIN

PROJECT TEAM

Client: **The Tate Gallery**
Architect: **James Stirling Michael Wilford & Associates**
Quantity Surveyor: **Davis Belfield & Everest**
John Dansken & Purdie
Structural Engineer: **W. G. Curtin & Partners**
Services Engineer: **Steensen, Varming, Mulcahy Partnership Ltd**

No single golden rule has been applied. Instead, all the many small choices that had to be made were made in intensive dialogue and with a high level of commitment from all those involved.

THE BLUECOAT

School Lane, Liverpool

Architect:	biq architecten
Construction Value:	£9.5 million
Completion Date:	March 2008
Project Type:	New-build arts wing, and restoration

^ Exterior view
PAUL MCMULLIN

Introduction

By 2001, the state of maintenance of the existing Bluecoat Chambers (which dates from 1717–25) was poor. Little had been done to the building after the wartime bomb-damage repairs in the 1950s. This meant that straightforward maintenance and repair was urgent, including repointing of brickwork, replacement of roof slates, repair of stonework, repair and maintenance of sash windows and maintenance of interior walls, floors and timberwork.

In addition, time had left its traces in the servicing of the building. The Bluecoat was a maze of old and new electric and telecom wires, gas, sewerage and water pipes.

In architectural terms, the building had largely lost its typological clarity. The central core had always been one open space – the ground floor had been used as a refectory, the upper floor as a chapel – and it was important that these central spaces continued to match this public aspect. However, this central core had become subdivided: the ground floor, for instance, contained a lobby, two corridors, a pair of galleries, a bookshop and a broom cupboard. The rear entrance to this part of the building was not through its axially positioned arched door but through a side entrance, leading to a confusing collection of corridors and stairs that made navigation difficult.

Client's Brief

The aims of the Bluecoat project were manifold; there was no such thing as a clear brief. In fact, the brief was formulated on the basis of a programmatic study that biq architecten made prior to commencing their design work.

The main driver of the operation was the need to make the entire building fully accessible, in compliance with the provisions of the Disability Discrimination Act (DDA)

2005. It was felt that an extension of the building would increase means to gain income, and this coincided with a long-felt desire to reinforce the Bluecoat within the cultural realm of the city of Liverpool.

The Bluecoat was keen to preserve its building, the oldest in Liverpool and highly appreciated by its inhabitants, within the new retail district to be formed by Liverpool One. The existing structure and the extension were treated as one singular building, underlining its somewhat sphinx-like properties in this new world of steel and glass with its obvious solidity of brickwork and stone.

Design Process

The project was centred around the following ambitions, encapsulating an integrated approach to the design:

Reciprocity

The new wing departed from the architectural properties (rather than the historical or heritage themes) of the existing monument:

- The urban typology of courts was restored.
- The new wing contains rooms rather than fluid (Modernist) space.
- Dominant materials, most notably brickwork, were continued.
- Proportions of windows, ridge heights and roofs were taken over from the existing building.
- The structural geometry was taken as an 'extrusion' of existing structures.

Some decisions in the design of the new wing informed interventions in the existing building:

- Bronze window frames were added where daylight was needed in the less-precious parts of the building.
- Skirtings and architraves in the interior continued from new into old.

∧ The Front elevation of The Bluecoat off School Lane
PAUL MCMULLIN

∧ Interior gallery space
PAUL MCMULLIN

- Oak floors continued from new into old.
- The colour palette (white, dark grey, natural timber) continued from new into old.

New looks old, old looks new. Stable architectural themes (type, structure, material, proportion and geometry) rather than temporary themes (such as design, colour and historical anecdotes) have defined the project.

Layering

The historic Bluecoat Chambers itself did not show architectural consistency. This was not taken as an alibi for an 'anything goes' modus operandi, but it did allow the extension to be defined as a new layer in the rich history of the Bluecoat. An example is the reading of the brickwork: the type of bricks themselves, the joints and the bonds all differed in each part of the building. The new wing has been constructed with loadbearing brickwork in wire-cut stack-bonded orange bricks – thus adding yet another, self-conscious layer to the palette of materials while staying close to the overall architectural vocabulary of the Bluecoat.

Extension

It was decided to use the extension for those programmatic items that were difficult to accommodate in the existing edifice: the performance and exhibition spaces. The volumes of these spaces were too large for the original building, and, moreover, current building codes required structural measures and the addition of new ventilation services that were almost impossible to integrate into an 18th-century shell.

Access nodes

Two new access nodes – providing lifts, stairs and ramps – were added where the different legs in the H-shaped plan meet. One of these was integrated into the new wing, the other one was inserted in the historic structure without demolishing or adversely affecting the oldest parts of the building.

Use

The topic of flexibility was discussed in depth. It was decided not to make neutral architectural spaces, in which 'everything and nothing' was possible. Instead, each space has a specific architectural character which 'provokes' use. In practice, this works very well – particularly in the curating of modern art, which so often is based on 'absent', white-cube architecture.

No single golden rule has been applied in the conversion of the Bluecoat. Instead, all the many small choices that had to be made were made in intensive dialogue and with a high level of commitment and concentration from all those involved.

Project Evaluation

The merits of the project may be best summarised by the praise it received from Portuguese architect Alvaro Siza, but in particular by his question: who was your client? In his experience, it is not at all obvious that art buildings are commissioned by their end user; of all the museums that Siza has built, this was the case only once – which in his view has had a negative effect on the buildings as places for art. Siza's admiration for the Bluecoat was equally about the design and the positive 'clientship' developed by its directors.

In dialogue with its funders, including Arts Council England, the Bluecoat was encouraged not to delegate the client's role to project managers but to take it on themselves and to define the design through their business case and functional needs. One of the reasons for selecting biq architecten was its ability to define projects from a real-estate perspective, to work with old buildings and their occupants and to combine a pragmatic outlook with a thorough understanding of historical and contemporary architecture. biq participated in the development of the brief and in the choice of the consultants and the project manager, who adopted a crucial facilitating role.

As a result, the Bluecoat is a building that works and is well liked by its users and visitors. This has been acknowledged by a range of publications and awards, including a nomination for the Mies van der Rohe Award 2008.

PROJECT TEAM

Client: **The Bluecoat**
Architect: **biq architecten, the Netherlands**
Executive Architect: **Austin-Smith:Lord LLP**
Conservation Architect: **Donald Insall Associates Ltd**
Main Contractor: **Kier North West**
Quantity Surveyor: **Tweeds**
Structural Engineer: **Techniker Ltd**
Services Engineer: **Griffiths**
Project Manager: **Buro Four**
Landscape Architect: **Austin-Smith:Lord LLP**
Interior and Furniture Designer: **biq architecten**
Acoustic Consultant: **Hoare Lea**
Access Consultant: **Buro Happold**

A PLACE TO LIVE

In the 1930s, Liverpool's population was over 800,000. By the 1990s this had halved, and the trend seemed ever downwards.

But this depopulation has now been halted, and there has been an increase in inward migration and retention of people born in the city. The massive improvements to the fabric of the city, the rise in broadly defined 'cultural' activities, and the firmer and more confident economic base are all reasons why people are happier to see Liverpool as home.

As a port city, Liverpool has always consisted in part of a transient population – indeed, this is one of its defining characteristics and the reason it remains a hub for innovation and creativity. As mercantile trade brought prosperity, new people brought a different type of currency – new ideas. In the late 20th century, Liverpool's economic and social breakdown led to the flight of many talented individuals and groups who were simply unable to deliver fully formed ideas and had to look elsewhere. Those that remained endured a period of confidence-sapping frustration. There was no question of the glass being 'half full' or 'half empty' – there was simply no glass.

As with many other cities, Liverpool has an 'inner core' of residential development dating from the Georgian period onwards, reflecting the huge population growth. The developments are almost geological in terms of what they tell us about periods of growth and the character of that growth, ranging from detached villas to row upon row of terraces. In some respects, these developments represent an escape from the sordid conditions prevalent in the city centre as Liverpool's commercial activity continued to expand, with the

^ Hope Place Georgian Housing
PAUL MCMULLIN

^ Canning Street
PAUL MCMULLIN

∨ Princes Park Housing
JOHN STONARD

vanguard of Georgian merchants establishing areas like
Canning on the ridge, well above the insalubrities of the
city centre.

The current success of the city centre housing market
is a reversal of this trend, with residents returning to
the centre at the expense of the housing inner core.
Areas such as Anfield and Breckfield in north Liverpool
have experienced market failure, and some 70,000 pre-
1919 terraced houses fall under the Housing Market
Renewal Initiative. Derelict and empty houses, and
sometimes whole streets, are clear signs of the decline
of Liverpool's population since the 1930's, and whilst
a programme for improvement has started to deliver
investment and renewal, there is still much to do. Whilst
it would be overly simplistic to refer to the healthy city
centre housing market and the degeneration of the
inner core as a strategic failure, the imbalance does
require intervention from both the public and private
sectors. The boarded up houses in some parts of the
inner core are a manifestation of just how far the city
fell, and the regeneration of these areas will be a true
test of the city's success.

The project demanded a highly imaginative and sensitive design approach in view of its location within a World Heritage Site and its position between the historic commercial port buildings and the Albert Dock.

^ Exterior
PAUL MCMULLIN

MANN ISLAND

Mann Island, Liverpool

Architect: Broadway Malyan Ltd
Construction Value: £120 million
Completion Date: Late 2011
Project Type: New-build

Introduction

Mann Island is a £120 million commercial mixed-use development, which sits at the heart of Liverpool's Maritime Mercantile World Heritage Site adjacent to the ensemble of Edwardian buildings known as the 'Three Graces'. Broadway Malyan was commissioned in early 2005 to produce proposals for the joint-venture clients, Neptune Developments and Countryside Properties.

The project arose following the collapse of the 'Fourth Grace' project, and the creation of a new site masterplan by Liverpool Vision, Liverpool City Council and the site owners, the Northwest Development Agency. The aim remained to deliver a vibrant, mixed-use development – incorporating residential, leisure and retail elements – that would contribute to the reanimation of the Liverpool waterfront and link the city centre with the Pier Head, Albert Dock and the new Museum of Liverpool.

The scheme consists of three buildings; three new public spaces, one of which is covered; a new canal basin; and extensive basement parking. It includes 376 apartments; a 13,000 m² net office building; 6,500 m² of retail and leisure space; and 1,200 m² of covered public space. After working closely with Liverpool City Council and gaining strong support from both CABE (the Commission for Architecture and the Built Environment) and English Heritage, a detailed planning consent was obtained in November 2006. Construction began in October 2007, and the scheme is due to be completed towards the end of 2011.

Client's Brief

In addition to its vibrant mix of uses, the brief stipulated that the development would have to create a series of public places and spaces – including a large, new, covered public-realm area – which could be used for a variety of formal and informal uses and activities. The project demanded a highly imaginative and sensitive design approach in view of its location within a World Heritage Site and its position between the historic commercial port buildings (the 'Three Graces') and the Albert Dock. An additional specific and important design requirement was the need to respect and conserve a series of key vistas of the 'Three Graces' that were considered essential to the visual ambience and character of the World Heritage Site.

The visual connection from the site back to the city was weak, with poor pedestrian legibility. The Strand, which is a busy multi-lane highway, forms a daunting physical and psychological barrier between the site and the city centre. A key challenge for the design was to overcome these issues and form a new pedestrian node, which would help reconnect the city centre to its riverfront and reanimate its once-thriving Pier Head and Albert Dock.

Design Process

The Mann Island scheme does not aim to continue the composition of the 'Three Graces', which sit over the former George's Dock – instead, its composition reflects the 'hinge point' in the urban grain. The geometry of its two residential 'wedges' relates to Mann Island and the Graving Docks, whilst the third, linear, commercial building relates to the geometry of The Strand and the city grid beyond.

Three new public spaces form a sequence, which will reconnect the city to its historic waterfront. A new public gathering space collects people from an enhanced Strand pedestrian crossing to the east, opening up views to the Albert Dock and providing public access to the George's Dock inlet. A glazed, covered public space between the two residential buildings links the area next to The Strand through to a sheltered south-facing public space around a new canal

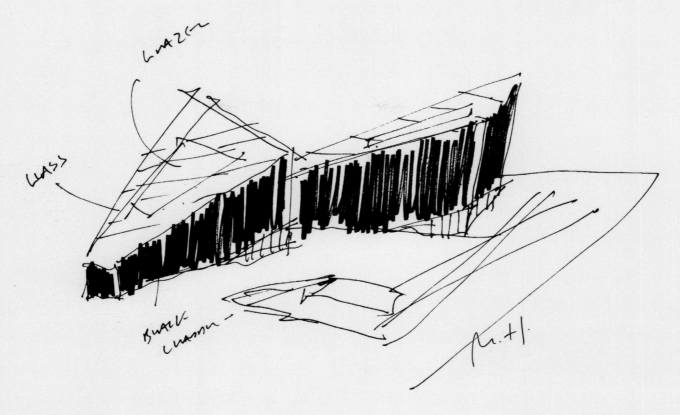

GLASS

GLAZED

BLACK GLAZED

v Exterior view
PAUL MCMULLIN

^ Original concept sketch, 2005
MATT BROOK

^ Architectural model
SUPPLIED BY BROADWAY MALYAN

basin. This covered area also provides the opportunity for exhibitions and information displays, thus acting as a 'foyer' to riverfront events. The space around the canal basin, defined by the residential buildings, will provide visitors with a unique, external, waterside leisure destination.

The lowest points of the two residential wedges are positioned to frame views through to the front and back elevations and roofscapes of the Pier Head group, whilst their apexes provide a visual draw and terminate key views along the pedestrian approaches from Chavasse Park to the southeast and the city centre to the east. The BREEAM 'Excellent' office building addresses views up and down The Strand and frames southern vistas through the George's Dock passage of the 'Three Graces'. An absolute-black polished-granite cladding to the residential wedges was chosen to reflect the foreground dock water and provide a clear visual contrast with the Pier Head group. The reflective nature of the granite was also selected to react to the rapidly changing lighting and weather conditions of the dock environment.

The scheme's fenestration is played down during the day, allowing the buildings to be read as large, pure forms on the quayside whilst providing a clear distinction between the new buildings and the visual intensity of the Pier Head group. The flush, polished granite-and-glass façades are intended to reflect the texture of the surrounding World Heritage Site, creating a changing appearance as visitors move through and around the buildings. Textured granite to the office building provides a backdrop to the profile of the residential wedges when viewed from the river.

These visually heavy buildings float over double-height, glazed retail-and-leisure podiums, whose projecting overhangs provide covered pedestrian routes around them. The glazed podiums also create a visual contrast to the solid bases of the adjacent 'Three Graces'. The sloping roofs of the residential wedges form 'fifth elevations', the roofscapes of which are animated with terraces providing residents with views of the river and surrounding World Heritage Site. This 'ribboned' roofscape also provides a sense of scale and texture, which is offset by the purity of the elevations.

Internally, the triangular plans of the residential buildings create two glazed atriums. The angle of their sloping roofscapes maximises sunlight penetration into the atriums and internal courtyard balconies, providing the north-facing apartments with a southern aspect. All the apartments are thus dual-aspect, and will benefit from the stack effect created by the atriums, which will provide them with natural cross-ventilation.

Project Evaluation

Despite the fact that the development has not yet been completed, the 'family' of three buildings is already seen as a unique addition to Liverpool's waterfront and its regeneration. Although there are opposing opinions in the city on the design of the buildings, and their fit with the iconic Pier Head group, there is little doubt that the buildings – including the 'wintergarden' and public space – will offer a new destination and bring further activity to this part of the city centre.

The view of the Pier Head group of buildings from the south has been changed as the Mann Island scheme takes shape, and the composition of the buildings

146

∨ CGI view from Salthouse Dock
UINIFORM

∨∨ Exterior view
PAUL MCMULLIN

∧ CGI
UNIFORM

across the site provides for glimpses of the towers and domes beyond rather than unobstructed views. In this respect, the scheme reflects pre-war views, with large, brick warehouses on the Mann Island site that also provided glimpsed views rather than wide vistas to the Pier Head.

PROJECT TEAM

Client: **Countryside Neptune LLP**
Architect: **Broadway Malyan Ltd**
Main Contractor: **BAM Construct UK Ltd**
Quantity Surveyor: **Tweeds**
Structural Engineer: **Bingham Davis Ltd**
Services Engineer: **Cundall Johnston and Partners LLP**
Cladding Specialist: **Weatherwise (Special Projects) Ltd**
Landscape Contractor: **English Landscapes Ltd**
Landscape Designer: **Broadway Maylan Ltd**

A 'tall-buildings cluster' had been envisaged for the CBD ever since the Shankland Masterplan for the city centre in the early 1960s.

^ View from Wallasey
PAUL MCMULLIN

BEETHAM
WEST TOWER

6–10 Brook Street, Liverpool

Architect:	Aedas
Construction Value:	£20 million
Completion Date:	Autumn 2007
Project Type:	New-build

Introduction

Beetham West Tower was built as the final phase of a major regeneration project at the former Liverpool Eye Hospital on a site fronted by Old Hall Street, which occupied an important, strategic location in Liverpool's central business district (CBD). The brief for the eye hospital site envisaged a mixture of uses, aiming to achieve an active and vibrant addition to the CBD in contrast to the earlier emphasis on office-led redevelopment schemes in the area. This was also a response to stronger city-centre residential demands in the property market at the time.

The initial masterplan for this triangular site included a 29-storey residential tower of 11,500 m2 at the northern apex of the plot, a 12-storey Radisson Hotel of 14,500 m2 with two basements, and a further seven-storey office building of 16,500 m2 – providing a total of 42,500 m2 of accommodation. West Tower was added to this ensemble following the acquisition of the remaining derelict building at the southwest corner of the site. The resulting 40-storey tower of 14,707 m2 encompasses five commercial floors with residential accommodation above, together with an elevated restaurant at the 34th level.

Client's Brief

Historically, the site occupied the most westerly end of the Leeds and Liverpool Canal, and had included a small dock office building. The latter was converted as a bar annexe to the Radisson Hotel.

A 'tall-buildings cluster' had been envisaged for the central business district ever since the Shankland Masterplan for the city centre in the early 1960s. Although the expectations in the brief were for a mix of buildings that included larger and broader forms of development augmented with elegant vertical towers giving variety and interest to Liverpool's skyline, the

latter failed to materialise in the initial development stages – primarily as a result of the preference for large office footprints in the development market. Recent success in achieving the tower form of development is mainly attributed to pressure from the residential market to take advantage of Liverpool's exciting panoramic views.

The restricted area of the site had an initial influence on the viability of its redevelopment. Further analysis of possible forms of development demonstrated the potential of a viable tall structure that could positively contribute to the city's skyline. The objective was also to extend the mixed-use redevelopment principle to this site, albeit within its limited area.

DesignProcess

Initial schemes for a modest three- to four-storey development on this site were considered. The proposals appeared insignificant and out of scale in relation to the volume of adjacent development, and overwhelmed by their exposure to a major highway artery into the city centre. The logic of expanding upwards was then examined; the location of a tall building on this plot appeared to offer an interesting termination to various long-distance vistas within the city and would consolidate the cluster of existing commercial towers and buildings in the Old Hall Street area.

The limited footprint of the site did help to deliver a structure of elegant proportions, and the rounded form of the resulting building took advantage of this in order to accentuate the tower's slender appearance. The design aimed to give a strong grounding to the building, which rises from pavement level on the main King Edward Street frontage. The plan form of the tower is orientated approximately north-east/south-east, in order to follow the same urban grid that defines the blocks in this part of the city, and therefore provides a strong

∧ Exterior from Princes Dock
PAUL MCMULLIN

∧ Interior of the Panoramic Restaurant on the 34th floor
SUPPLIED BY ARCHITECT

axial view of the River Mersey.

The glazed curtain-walling finish to the apartment levels was developed to provide subtlety in pattern and texture; this lent the building a degree of richness in finish. The elevations are clad in a high-quality fully glazed perimeter wall of randomly juxtaposed clear and opaque panels, faceted to form the curved elevations. These units contrast with the simple grid of regular, frameless panels of opaque glazing – punctuated by stair windows and louvres – which clad the service core. The latter rises through all levels of the development, accommodating the lifts, stair and mechanical services. Its location to the rear of the tower, facing the adjacent offices, avoids any overlooking issues and forms a slim vertical element that is flanked by the clear and opaque apartment windows, whose random arrangement avoids a horizontal layering effect.

The apartments are orientated to provide maximum views of both the city and river, whilst the glazing facing the adjacent office buildings is minimised in order to restrict direct overlooking between buildings.

The lower five floors of offices are set back between columns, and are fully glazed to provide an 'animated façade' at street level. A glazed stair, with a backdrop of bright yellow and views to the river, is accommodated between raking fins.

The termination of the tower was also carefully considered in order to address the panoramic views of the city from the river – as well as the various inland vistas available at that height. The upper apartments are tiered back to provide external terraces, which are backlit to provide a crown-like glow at night and have become a distinctive addition to the Liverpool skyline.

West Tower is confidently planned to provide a slim, elegant profile, and utilises contemporary materials to maximise the potential for views and daylight for its occupants whilst minimising its visual impact upon its neighbours.

Project Evaluation

Although the design of Beetham West Tower did initially attract criticism – especially from some quarters, in which it was seen as a case of overdevelopment on a restricted city-centre site – the overwhelming majority now welcomes the building as a successful addition to Liverpool's skyline.

As the tallest building in the CBD, the tower fits well amongst the former's new tall-buildings cluster. The building's slender appearance gives it a pleasing elegance that tends to elude many other similar developments for which commercial success is a prime consideration. The building won the distinction of 'best mixed-use development of the year' at the Regional Property Awards in April 2008.

PROJECT TEAM

Client: **The Beetham Organization Ltd**
Architect: **Aedas**
Main Contractor: **Carillion plc**
Quantity Surveyor: **Turner & Townsend**
Structural Engineer: **Latham Consulting**
Services Engineer: **Buro Happold**
Project Manager: **The Beetham Organization Ltd**
Fire Engineering: **FEDRA**
Window and Cladding Technology Consultant: **Wintech Limited**

It is the careful marrying of modern design with the grandeur of the Elmes school building that initially attracted the residents.

^ Exterior view on Shaw Street
PAUL MCMULLIN

THE COLLEGIATE

Shaw Street, Everton, Liverpool

Architect:	shedkm architects
Construction Value:	£9 million
Completion Date:	November 2001
Project Type:	Regeneration

Introduction

The Grade II* listed Collegiate School, originally designed by Harvey Lonsdale Elmes (the architect of Liverpool's St George's Hall) in 1843, is an imposing Neo-Gothic sandstone structure in Everton on the edge of Liverpool city centre. A much-loved local icon, the school was the centrepiece of the Shaw Street Conservation Area – numbering among its neighbours the church of St Francis Xavier, the Particular Baptist Church and the late Georgian terraces lining Shaw Street itself.

Since its final closure as a school in 1985 the building had suffered extensive fire damage, and numerous unrealised refurbishment schemes had failed to reconcile the substantial regeneration costs with a new use. Finally, a catastrophic Bonfire Night blaze in 1994 destroyed much of the remaining internal structure, leaving the building in a precarious state and perilously close to collapse.

The condition of the Collegiate was in many ways representative of the dramatic fall in status of the Everton area of the city, which had once been a Georgian suburb. Its adaptive reuse has led to a number of the houses in the Georgian terraces of Shaw Street being restored, and has given a new impetus to regeneration locally.

Client's Brief

In 1997, newly formed architectural practice shedkm architects were asked by new owners Urban Splash to look at a more radical regeneration solution, which many commentators regarded as the building's last chance.

shedkm's proposal was to transform the school into 95 one- and two-bedroom apartments. Through an approach of considered 'discerning conservation', only the most important parts of the existing buildings were preserved – with elements of lesser quality, or those that had suffered particularly severe damage, being stripped away. The latter included the original rear elevation – built not of stone but of brick, and allegedly not even designed by Elmes but by the City Surveyor following a disagreement over the architect's fees.

Hence, the massive stone façades to the front and sides were retained and carefully repaired, and, with the unsafe rear elevation and internal walls and floors removed, a complete remodelling of the building interior was made possible. With a new rear elevation and roofscape, the Collegiate regeneration is in effect a new building sitting within the existing stonework. A similar approach has been applied to the school's octagonal theatre, which has been thereby transformed into a walled communal garden.

Design Process

Each apartment has been carefully tailored to fit its position within the existing footprint. The primary axis – running through from the grand main entrance, staircase and link to the garden – has been retained and strengthened with new elements and a huge glass wall, which allows views into the garden from the circulation areas.

Particular care has been taken to ensure a clear distinction between existing and new construction, an approach that is carried through from a strategic level down to the detailing. The sensitivity of this approach was key in securing both support and funding from English Heritage.

The apartments on the first three floors are planned around dramatic double-height living spaces that accommodate the 5 m-high existing windows of the front and side façades, whilst the rear units echo this arrangement but focus on new openings and external balconies. Apartments are defined by the layout of the new cross-walls, the 'cranked' design not only giving the new structure stability but also containing the staircases to the apartments' upper levels. Bedrooms are lifted onto a gallery level in order to give privacy, but open to the double-height living space. Kitchen and bathroom modules are tightly planned around vertical service cores, and push out into the common areas – adding a touch of rhythm to the once-institutional central corridor. Utility and storage areas are tucked behind simple wall planes, to maintain the open plan, with a series of sliding doors offering further enclosure when appropriate.

The delicate stone tracery of the existing windows was not compatible with modern glazing requirements, and so new full-height glass 'boxes' are set back from the façade, creating in turn a small wintergarden for each apartment. At the top of the building penthouses, fully glazed walls – pulled respectfully back from the restored, castellated stone parapet – open onto terraces with views across Liverpool, the Mersey estuary and the North Wales mountains.

Behind the main building, the separate octagonal theatre has been extensively remodelled, with only the external walls retained and stabilised by a new high-level steel plane. A garden deck has been introduced at first-floor level, and is divided by an exposed-concrete ramp rising from a bridge that connects back into the main building entrance lobby and carefully restored grand staircase. At the top of this stair sits a huge fireplace, recovered from the headmaster's rooms and painstakingly restored.

In the garden, mature Himalayan birch trees and Virginia creepers fill the space with greenery which is visible through window openings from the rear apartments and to passers-by outside. The walled garden provides a tranquil amenity space of the kind that is often lacking in city-centre developments.

Following planning permission and listed building consent in early 1998, demolition and stonework restoration commenced in June of that year. The first three show apartments were opened in October 2000, with final completion a year later.

Project Evaluation

The Collegiate was among the first wave of new city-centre residential developments in Liverpool. It is interesting to hear from long-term owner-occupiers, who constitute the majority of residents, that it is the careful marrying of modern design with the grandeur of the Elmes school building that initially attracted them – and that has kept them there, despite competition from the many other apartment schemes subsequently built in the city. Importantly, the apartments are unique to the building, with new elements a direct response to the existing fabric but designed to complement the scale of Elmes's original design.

The Collegiate Old Boys Society have held their AGM in the refurbished building on a number of occasions, and the architects are still in contact with the residents'

^ Top floor apartment and balcony space
HUFTON + CROW

management committee who now maintain the building, advising on ongoing care for the fabric.

The Collegiate's regeneration has been a catalyst for other, sorely needed developments in the area – a part of the city that had seen rapid depopulation and decline, leaving many fine Victorian buildings in a state of neglect. The Collegiate is an important Liverpool landmark, and its regeneration was seen as a symbol of the wider resurgence of the city. This, together with the quality of the design, has been recognised by a series of accolades including Housing Design, RIBA and Civic Trust awards.

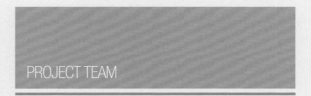

PROJECT TEAM

Client: **Urban Splash Limited**
Architect: **shedkm architects**
Main Contractors: **Totty Construction Group Ltd,**
Heyrod Construction, Maysand Ltd
Quantity Surveyor: **Simon Fenton Partnership LLP**
Structural Engineer: **Curtins Consulting**
Services Engineer: **Steven A. Hunt & Associates**

The architects' bold design approach in developing buildings of individual character and distinctive form on a tight city-centre site is refreshing to see.

^ Exterior
MCCOY WYNNE

EDEN SQUARE

Hatton Garden, Liverpool

Architect: Arkheion
Construction Value: £20 million
Completion Date: December 2007
Project Type: Combination of conversion and new-build

Introduction

Eden Square is built on a site spanning Hatton Garden and Cheapside, and sandwiched between the Grade II* listed Main Bridewell, the Grade II listed former Central Fire Station buildings to the south and the former GPO parcel office building to the north. The site falls within the Castle Street Conservation Area, and was assembled by the clients for a mixed-use development project.

This has involved the demolition of the remainder of a late Victorian frontage to Hatton Garden, which had been partly torn down in the 1930s for the development of the parcel-sorting office building. The latter was recently converted for residential purposes. The remnant had a somewhat utilitarian post-war extension to its rear, built on what was originally the service yard of the GPO building.

The scheme was designed to permit pedestrian permeability through the site, and it incorporates two new buildings: a ten-storey structure fronting Hatton Garden, and another – thirteen storeys in height – facing Cheapside. These are primarily residential, with commercial accommodation at ground- and first-floor levels. They provide 123 apartments and commercial accommodation.

The designers strove to strike a balance between conformity with the site's historical character and the animation of the street scene, with some individual and striking new-build forms.

Client's Brief

The scheme provided the opportunity to inject new life and vibrancy into the heart of an area that had suffered obsolescence owing to a total change in its economic profile.

To that end, the brief was to seek improvements to access and permeability through the site, aiming to provide an attractive and accessible public realm. The brief was also guided by the City Centre Vision Framework, which foresaw the regeneration of this area as a live/work quarter and responded to strong market demands at the time for residential accommodation in the city centre.

As a result, active ground-floor uses were sought in order to animate the public realm and attract pedestrian movement through the site as part of a lateral east–west route traversing the blocks between Dale Street and Tithebarn Street.

The specific design challenges were to provide a sensitive insertion into an established city-centre fabric, which nonetheless demonstrated strong regeneration confidence and outlook. The scheme was also to contribute positively in its skyline to distant views from important vantage points, such as that from nearby St John's Garden.

Design Process

As with many other city-centre schemes, at Eden Square detailed analysis was carried out of the maximum acceptable building height for the proposals. This led to successive permutations and adjustments – both to the overall design and to the form of each of the scheme's constituent structures.

The architects adopted different design aesthetics for the two new buildings, derived from the particular geometry of their sites and their street exposure. The new buildings were designed as freestanding glazed towers, giving greater freedom in the development of their forms. An elliptical footprint was chosen for Eden Square East, the block with a Hatton Garden frontage, inviting gentle sweeping access into the site.

^ Exterior
MCCOY WYNNE

^ Exterior
MCCOY WYNNE

By contrast, the pedestrian route from Cheapside runs through a dramatic, narrow vertical gap, responding to the tighter street grain to the opposite end of the site where the stepped form of Eden Square West takes over.

Building form also responded to the circulation patterns in and around the site, aiming to achieve an interesting juxtaposition of building blocks that would present a pleasing visual experience to pedestrians traversing the route through the site.

The two buildings share a monochromatic choice of finishing materials, lending the scheme some unified identity. A grey terracotta-cladding finish was selected which blends well with the imposing, Classically styled Portland stone portico of the former GPO building and the stone dressing of the listed fire station flanking both sides of Eden Square's Hatton Garden frontage.

Project Evaluation

The architects' bold design approach in developing buildings of individual character and distinctive form on a tight city-centre site is refreshing to see. The synthesis of built forms responding to movement, circulation and spatial flow also contributes to the dynamism of the scheme.

A successful landscaping design was implemented for the public areas of the development, sympathetic to the buildings' aesthetics. Although inevitably affected by the current severe economic downturn, it is hoped that the completion of the conversion/redevelopment of the neighbouring properties to the south of the site will provide the all-important 'critical mass' of active floorspace necessary for the intended 'active and vibrant' public realm to really take off at Eden Square. Unfortunately, a strategy of gating the access route – partly, it must be said, in contravention of a planning condition – has to some extent undermined the intended permeability of the development.

Nonetheless, the Eden Square development has successfully integrated into its urban context, and its amplified scale in relation to the general building height in the Conservation Area does not appear overpowering. The scheme's distant silhouette adds an interesting new layer to the views from St John's Garden and Crosshall Street. Conversely, the project's high-level accommodation affords equally fascinating, panoramic views of the city's townscape, which are much appreciated by residents.

PROJECT TEAM

Client: **Downing Developments**
Architect: **Arkheion**
Main Contractor: **George Downing Construction**
Quantity Surveyor: **George Downing Construction**
Structural Engineer: **Alan Johnston Partnership**
Services Engineer: **Teknikal Design Services**
Project Manager: **Downing Property Services**
Acoustic Consultant: **BDP Acoustics**

153

Campbell Square blends historic buildings with contemporary design to create a vibrant inner-city community.

^ Campbell Square with Bridewell
PAUL MCMULLIN

CAMPBELL SQUARE

Campbell Street and Henry Street, Liverpool

Architects: Brock Carmichael Associates
Construction Value: £21 million
Completion Date: August 2002
Project Type: New-build, conversion and public realm

Introduction

A prestigious mixed-use regeneration development in the heart of historic Liverpool, Campbell Square blends historic buildings with contemporary design to create a vibrant inner-city community, in which people can live, work and visit in a safe and attractive environment.

The Campbell Square development was created on a site at the lower end of Duke Street. Bounded by Argyle Street, York Street and Duke Street, and close to the Albert Dock, the plot lay within the Duke Street Conservation Area – later part of Liverpool's historic Ropewalks district. The site covered 1.2 ha and featured surviving 18th-, 19th- and early 20th-century commercial and domestic buildings, including five listed structures – most notably, a former police bridewell that had served the docks – and the unlisted Ayrton Saunders Laboratory building.

The development provides a wide choice of residential accommodation, ranging from 'loft' conversions in refurbished listed warehouses, to modern apartments, duplexes and luxury penthouses. At the heart of the scheme is Campbell Square, a new open space and focal point incorporating kinetic lighting, 'boxed' hornbeam trees and a new public artwork, 'The Seed'.

Client's Brief

The brief for this diverse scheme requested 128 residential units, 1,200 m² of offices and 3,482 m² of business space, as well as three bars and restaurants together with a new public square from which the scheme takes it name.

Key objectives were:

- to remove dereliction and improve the quality of the environment;
- to restore the listed buildings and bring them back into productive use;

- to demolish obsolete poor-quality buildings and construct new ones of high design quality and appropriate to the context;
- to develop cleared sites and re-establish the street frontages;
- to create a new public space with a distinctive character and identity;
- to deter illegal parking and 'rat running' of cars through the area; and
- to reduce crime and vandalism.

The difficult problem of finding solutions for the dilapidated historic listed buildings, which would bring them back into productive reuse and achieve an appropriate standard of architectural conservation, was assisted by the securing of Heritage Lottery funding under the first round of the Townscape Heritage Initiative.

Design Process

Cruden Construction acted as the principal design-and-build contractor for the design and construction of all works.

The new scheme built on the strong architectural heritage of the area, ensuring that the sensitive refurbishment of the existing structures was integrated with the new-build elements. Several existing buildings were demolished, whilst others were retained and incorporated into the development.

The main commercial office space occupied a prime position facing Duke Street and offering 3,100 m² of space over five storeys, complete with basement car parking for 29 vehicles. Its construction comprised bulk basement excavation, contiguous piling, a structural steel frame, composite steel-and-concrete 'multi-deck' floors, standing-seam stainless-steel and aluminium roofs, facing brick and anti-sun curtain walling, and powder-coated aluminium windows. The building was finished to shell standard, with core services installation comprising two passenger lifts, air-conditioning throughout, raised access floors, revolving entrance door, disabled access provision to all suites, toilets to each floor and essential heating and electrical services.

Residential and leisure elements were created in both the refurbished and the new buildings, with the residential blocks offering a range of apartment types and sizes. A variety of construction techniques was employed, and external finishes varied from building to building. Restored brickwork and new-build brown-brick elevations, blue slate, existing grey slate and aluminium roofs, rendered panels around windows, Georgian-style softwood and aluminium windows, blast-cleaned and painted exposed steelwork, double-glazed curtain walling, steel balconies, and stainless-steel and glass canopies all featured in order to present a modern, contemporary look to the finished scheme that nonetheless successfully blended old with new. Throughout the development, Cruden took great care to restore and reuse materials saved during demolitions or contained within conserved structures. Extensive consultation with English Heritage resulted in sensitive restoration of the various listed buildings.

Internally, the apartments feature fully fitted kitchens and bathrooms. Leisure units were completed to shell standard only, in order to allow for tenant fit-out.

External works included the formation of the new Campbell Square, using a mixture of hard and soft landscaping, and roads and pathways specified to

Liverpool City Council adoptable standards. The new space also incorporated sensitively designed street lighting and the erection of street-art sculptures.

In 2008, during Liverpool's year as European Capital of Culture, the square featured on the 'Go Superlambananas' trail, and hosted several of the best models of the Superlambanana, Liverpool's most iconic modern sculpture.

Project Evaluation

Campbell Square is a unique development, which has restored life to a previously derelict environment – in the process saving several pieces of historical architecture and creating a diverse, mixed-use community in the heart of Liverpool. The introduction of new uses led to improved market confidence in the area, and helped to support the existing local economy and enhance property values.

This pioneering scheme acted as a catalyst for several subsequent developments nearby, such as the Artists' Village and Cleveland Square, and both Cruden Construction and Brock Carmichael are proud of the part they played in its success.

The quality of the development has been recognised by its receiving a number of awards, including winner of the Best Urban Heritage Project and joint winner of the Planning Achievement category in the Royal Town Planning Institute (RTPI) North West Region Planning Achievement Awards 2002; it also won Best Regeneration Scheme in the Roses Design Awards 2002 and a RENEW Exemplar Award for Originality & Innovation in Regeneration 2004.

The judges' citation for the RTPI awards stated: 'Members of the judging panel were impressed by the quality of regeneration work and attention to detail, which was considered to be truly exceptional'.

∨ Campbell Square detail
JOHN STONARD

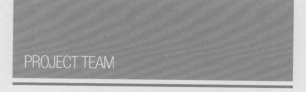

PROJECT TEAM

Client: **The Beetham Organization Ltd**
Architect: **Brock Carmichael Associates**
Main Contractor: **Cruden Construction Limited**
Quantity Surveyor: **Youdan Briggs Ltd**
Structural Engineer (Buildings 1, 2, 5; D, F):
Latham Hosseini Partnership
Structural Engineer (Buildings 3, 4, 6; A, C, E):
Roger Hetherington & Associates
Services Engineer: **Miller Walmsley Partnership**
Project Manager: **Peter Lorimer Associates**
Landscape Architect: **BCA Landscape**
Public Art: **Stephen Broadbent Artworks Limited**

^ The Picton Reading Room
PAUL MCMULLIN

A PLACE TO LEARN

It is entirely appropriate that there should be a section on a place to learn in a book about contemporary architecture in Liverpool.

The first school of architecture to be established in the UK – in 1895 – was in Liverpool, closely followed by the university's Department of Civic Design. Early professors in the field of the built environment were Patrick Abercrombie and Charles Reilly – figures of enormous influence, not just at the time but also in the manner in which they pioneered design teaching.

< Liverpool Institute
of Performing Arts
(LIPA)
PAUL MCMULLIN

∧ Art & Design Academy with Metropolitan Cathedral of Christ the King
PAUL MCMULLIN

With three universities and some 50,000 students, the city is a popular place to study. The rise in student numbers has been attributed not only to the popularity of the courses on offer but also to the city itself. There is little evidence of 'town and gown' conflict in a city in which education is valued – any city that has an active Philosophy in Pubs group is unlikely to adopt an 'us and them' approach to student visitors. In any case, that is not the Liverpool way – this is a city that is used to visitors and to people from other cultures, and all three universities are seeking to attract even more overseas students. Some of this activity has led to ill-considered and poor-quality developments, such as the student accommodation adjacent to Lime Street Station, but both the city and the universities are now working together to deliver well-designed and high-specification residences.

Design excellence in our schools and universities is crucial in both attracting students and providing stimulating surroundings. New buildings such as the Art and Design Academy, with its thoughtful approach and adaptable spaces, are not just fit for purpose but are also inspiring places in which to learn. The University of Liverpool Engineering Building illustrates how a dull and uninspiring

^^ Kind Seed Centre on back Canning Street
PAUL MCMULLIN

^ Sydney Jones Library , University of Liverpool
PAUL MCMULLIN

> School of Tropical
Medicine
PAUL MCMULLIN

> Interior of Art and
Design Academy
PAUL MCMULLIN

original design can be dynamically transformed, whilst The Aldham Robarts Learning Resource Centre has done much to enliven its surrounding area and provide a new impetus for regeneration. The Academy of St Francis of Assisi is more than just a new school: with sustainability as a core element of the curriculum, the building instructs by example and illustrates that the subject is not only worthy, but educational.

In investing in its educational buildings, in creating buildings that are dramatic and intriguing, Liverpool is investing in itself.

159

The academy was envisaged as an opportunity to raise the aspirations of the school, to provide a fuller range of activities and to strike a balance between craft-based skills and new technologies.

∧ Reflection of 'Paddy's Wigwam' in the window
PAUL MCMULLIN

> Exterior view
PAUL MCMULLIN

LIVERPOOL JOHN MOORES UNIVERSITY ART AND DESIGN ACADEMY

2 Duckinfield Street, Liverpool

Architect: Rick Mather Architects
Construction Value: £19.5 million
Completion Date: January 2009
Project Type: New-build

Introduction

The firm of Rick Mather Architects was selected, via a process of competitive interview, by Liverpool John Moores University to design their new Art and Design Academy on a site adjacent to a major Liverpool landmark: the Metropolitan (Roman Catholic) Cathedral of Christ the King.

Despite such an iconic neighbour, the Art and Design Academy was conceived as a landmark building in its own right, and it aims to ensure that the university, and future generations of its students, continues to play an influential role in the creative arts – both in the region and nationally.

The building is the first of a series of planned investments by Liverpool John Moores University (LJMU) in the area, and as such was required to set the quality-design benchmark for later phases of development. This not only included a level of architectural excellence, but also a new north–south pedestrian route across the site in order to allow for greater ease of movement between the university buildings and adjoining areas of the city centre.

Client's Brief

The university sought to procure, from a restrained budget, a high-quality building that was intended to meet their academic requirements and raise the profile for a new campus. The building instigates the first phase of a campus masterplan-realisation strategy, setting the standard for future developments across the university.

Founded in 1825 as the Liverpool Mechanics' School of Arts, LJMU's School of Art and Design is the oldest such institution in the UK outside London. The school's premises were previously spread across a number of buildings, which, at the time that a new building was mooted, were deemed no longer fit for purpose.

The university's vision for the new academy was to bring all of their art and design programmes together in a stimulating new space – enabling more creative forms of teaching and research to flourish, and offering new facilities and services to the region's creative-industries business sector. Public accessibility to the new facilities and the maximising of interaction between staff, students and associated businesses was another major objective for the new building.

The academy was envisaged as an opportunity to raise the aspirations of the school, to provide a fuller range of activities and to strike a balance between craft-based skills and new technologies.

Design Process

The building was conceived as a serpentine form which bends and curves to reflect the shape of the site, aligning primarily with the base of the cathedral. Its orientation provides a generous open space between the two buildings, which will be landscaped to provide a new public green space and to facilitate the commissioning of site-specific artwork.

The building's sculptural form is emphasised by the splayed blade-like windows, which maximise natural light from the north while its solid walls offer shade from strong, direct sunlight during midday hours.

The main entrance aligns with the west axis of the cathedral. Spanning three storeys, it draws students, staff and visitors into the central atrium, the social heart of the building. This space encourages interaction between the different disciplines and public facilities, with a dramatic open staircase rising up through the atrium and connecting to all levels. The extensive use of glass floods the academy with light, opening it up to viewers both inside and outside the building.

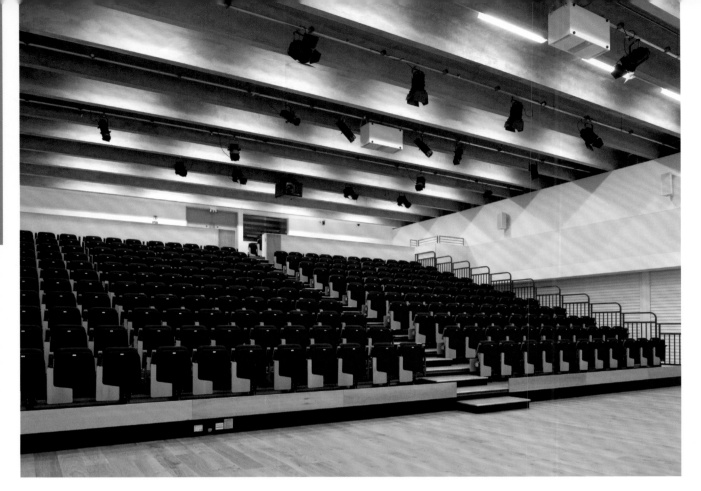

^ Interior of lecture theatre
PAUL MCMULLIN

The 11,000 m² of floor space is distributed over six levels, with the upper storeys set back to respond to key views from the cathedral and to create tiered roof terraces offering outstanding views across the city. The lower-ground and ground floors provide shared facilities, including the Tate Café, seminar rooms, a 350-seat multi-purpose space, galleries and exhibition spaces, which are also used for public and corporate events.

Studios and teaching spaces have been designed to be as flexible as possible, maximising daylight, space and energy-efficiency – and offering wireless access to computing technology throughout. The academy offers multi-disciplinary spaces where students of fine art, graphic arts, product design, interior design, architecture, fashion and textiles can interact with each other, share ideas and embark on new creative journeys together.

The use of off-white bricks and lime mortar was selected to provide a homogeneous external appearance which reflects the colour and tone of the stone used on the cathedral. Metal cladding was used to signify the top-floor studio 'pavilion', which is also used for events outside the main teaching periods.

The structure, mechanical and electrical services, accessibility and acoustics have been at the heart of the design throughout the building's development and realisation.

The high-quality concrete columns and soffits are left exposed in the teaching spaces in order to maximise the thermal mass of the building, which 'dampens', and reduces the possibility of, rapid temperature fluctuation, and creates a comfortable environment throughout the year.

The mechanical and electrical design limits the demand for fossil fuels by using passive design techniques and installing the most energy-efficient technologies. Maximising the daylight to the studios and seminar rooms minimises the need to use carbon-intensive electrical energy. Automated windows in the teaching spaces are linked back to the building management system (BMS) and activate as part of the ventilation system of the building.

The academy has achieved a BREEAM rating of 'Very Good' in accordance with the university's requirements, incorporating renewable energy sources such as a biomass heating system.

Project Evaluation

The building was occupied in January 2009, and has already successfully raised the expectations of its staff and students. The 2009 Degree Shows were the first public events to be held throughout the building, allowing the general public their first opportunity to visit the new academy. Full operation of the public gallery and exhibition spaces commenced in the summer of 2009, with a planned programme of exhibitions and events.

The Tate Café has been operating effectively in the building from the start of 2009, catering for all events associated with the academy. Large conference events have already successfully taken place, with major organisations such as the BBC providing high praise for the building and its facilities.

Liverpool John Moores University has been encouraged, by the high design quality of this building, to pursue

a policy of commissioning architectural excellence in other schemes planned for the future throughout their city-wide portfolio. The building has also been a major catalyst in helping both the public and private sectors to fund schemes within the area, based on new development and public-realm works. These are helping to regenerate and reanimate this part of the city centre, and to enhance the access and setting of the Metropolitan Cathedral.

PROJECT TEAM

Client: **Liverpool John Moores University**
Architect: **Rick Mather Architects**
Main Contractor: **Wates Construction**
Quantity Surveyor: **Turner & Townsend**
Structural Engineer: **Ramboll UK Ltd**
Services Engineer: **Ramboll UK Ltd**
Project Manager: **Davis Langdon LLP**
Acoustic Engineer: **Sandy Brown Associates**
Access Consultant: **Buro Happold**

163

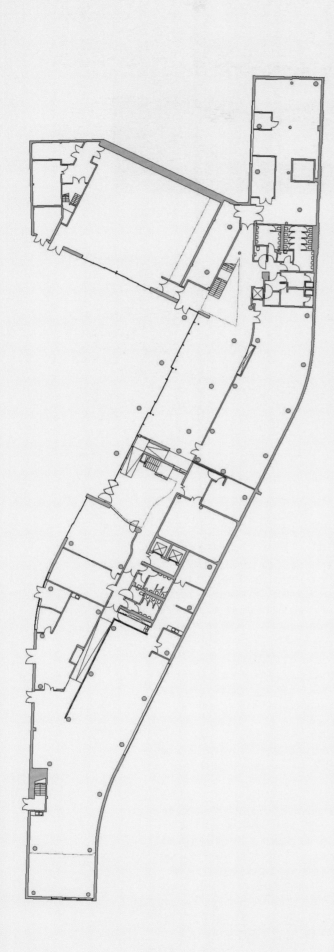

The Active Learning Lab
was conceived as a studio-
based teaching environment
for engineers, which would
regenerate the run-down
laboratory-building complex
within the campus and provide
a beacon for teaching and
learning.

UNIVERSITY OF LIVERPOOL ENGINEERING RESTRUCTURING PROJECT

Department of Engineering, Brownlow Hill, Liverpool

Architect:	Sheppard Robson
Construction Value:	£19 million
Completion Date:	December 2008
Project Type:	Refurbishment, adaptations and new extensions

Introduction

The Liverpool skyline is characterised by a number of significant structures representing the city's culture, institutions and heritage: the Liver Building (commerce), St John's Tower (retail and power) and the cathedrals (faith). These landmarks help seafarers to identify the city from some distance away. They also act as orientating devices within the city centre – both physically and psychologically – marking the varied 'quarters' or facets of Liverpool society.

The University of Liverpool's Department of Engineering enjoys a magnificent location at the peak of Brownlow Hill, strategically adjacent to the original Victoria Building (which gave its name to 'redbrick universities' everywhere) and 'Paddy's Wigwam' – the Cathedral of Christ the King, designed by Sir Frederick Gibberd and built on the foundation of Sir Edwyn Lutyens's original cathedral crypt. It also straddles the rail main tunnels which were cut through sandstone tens of metres below during the Victorian era, in order to link Lime Street Station with Manchester and London.

The Active Learning Lab (ALL) was conceived as a studio-based teaching environment for engineers, which would regenerate the run-down laboratory-building complex within the campus and provide a beacon for teaching and learning at the university – visible from the city centre, and even from out to sea.

Client's Brief

The catalyst for the project was the university's 'Liverpool Engineer' mission statement. This contained the new concept of an 'active learning laboratory' as a focus of engineering activity, bringing together teaching and research and linking these to the remainder of the university and to the city of Liverpool. The laboratory was to accommodate the full engineering process –

from conception and design, through fabrication and assembly to testing – in a single facility.

The university's engineering department was dispersed across a number of existing premises on campus, with no effective focus and difficult circulation patterns between buildings. The brief called for this situation to be rationalised, with the Active Learning Lab facilities as a central element.

The ALL was seen as an iconic structure: an identifiable landmark to act as a high-profile new 'face' of engineering, and as a powerful tool in attracting students and staff. Its landmark status would be reinforced by the prominent site near the original heart of the university.

The brief called for the retention and adaptation of the department's historic buildings, including the original Victorian Walker Building and the later Edwardian Harrison Hughes Building. It also stipulated continuation of the department's research work during the construction process, involving the retention of certain research facilities and minimal decanting of others.

Design Process

The evaluation of various options against the client's brief led to a design which was based on the retention and refurbishment or adaptation of many of the existing buildings concerned – including the historic structures identified in the brief, but also extending to the link block and podium facing Brownlow Hill. These last two structures comprised extensions from the 1960s, and the podium formed the base for the Mechanical Engineering Tower which rises to seven storeys in height. The latter was to be demolished in order to make way for the Active Learning Lab, which was to be constructed above the existing accommodation. Extensions into the courtyard at the rear of the podium and link were discounted, owing to restrictions arising from this area having been

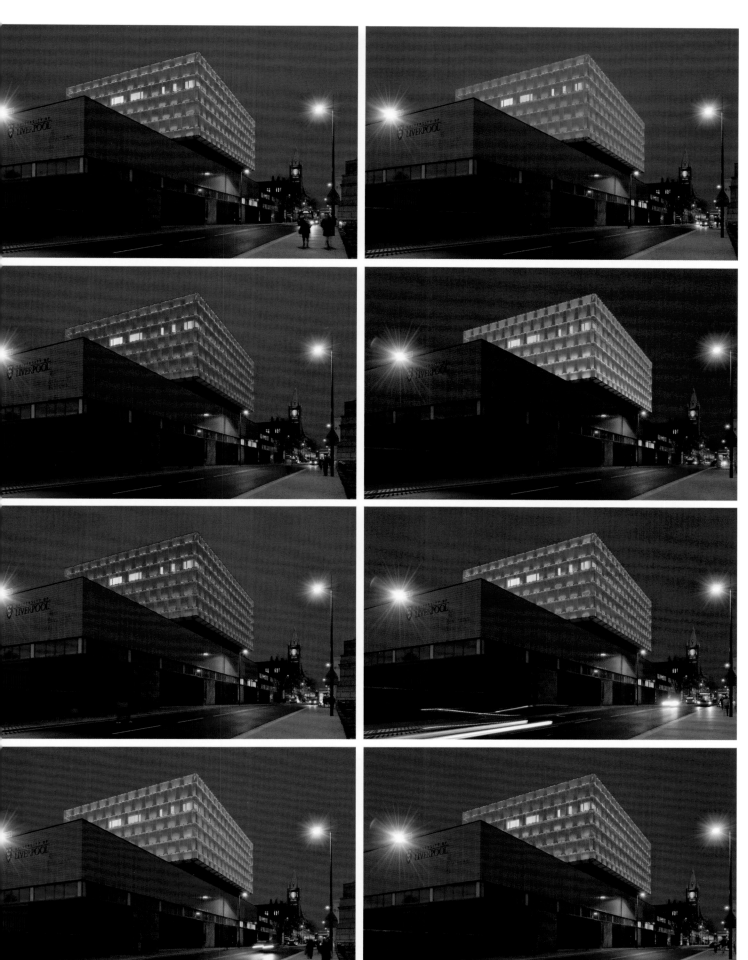

constructed as a deck above the railway cutting on the main lines into Lime Street Station.

The existing laboratories and boiler house behind the Walker and Harrison Hughes Buildings were demolished in order to accommodate a new glazed circulation element, or 'Street', intended to link together all the existing buildings, including each of their differing floor levels. The Street was designed as the heart of the department, having clearly visible circulation routes combined with display and break-out facilities. At the same time, the design included a new single entrance into the department, in order to replace the separate entrances into each existing building and to lead directly from the main historic University Quadrangle into the Street.

In form, the ALL has been developed as a glass-faced cube floating above the existing podium. This effect has been achieved by the use of a bespoke glass rainscreen cladding system on the outside face of its external wall. The external wall itself is composed of lightweight insulated cladding with a liquid-applied membrane facing, and it incorporates individual windows rather than continuous glazing. This approach ingeniously combines the need for restricted glazing areas in the laboratories with the 'landmark' appearance of a glass box. The glass rainscreen panels alternate between clear and fritted glazing, with adjoining panels offset in plan and section in order to introduce a rhythm to each façade. The panels overlap each other, and in doing so produce patterns of reflections across the building elevations. The university has undertaken the installation of an external lighting scheme for the ALL. This scheme uses LED-based luminaires, allowing the possibility of

∧ CGI exterior of the rear
COURTESY OF ARCHITECTS

programmable colour designs and positioned so that
the frit pattern on the glazing picks up the light in order
to give the effect of a glowing façade.

Project Evaluation

Whilst the building has not yet been occupied long
enough to provide a meaningful project evaluation,
it has already begun to prove influential within its
institutional context. The University of Liverpool is now
undertaking a far-reaching programme of public-realm
works, including the nearby University Square, as part
of a partnership approach to enhancing the whole of
Liverpool's knowledge quarter. It is also investing in
refurbishing existing buildings and developing new
teaching and residential blocks. The significance of the
Active Learning Lab project so far has been its seminal
value in fixing high-quality design as a prime objective
in subsequent projects.

∨ Daylight detail of panels
PAUL MCMULLIN

PROJECT TEAM

Client: **The University of Liverpool**
Architect: **Sheppard Robson**
Main Contractor: **BAM Construction Ltd (formerly HBG) – North
West**
Quantity Surveyor: **Capita Symonds**
Structural Engineer: **Arup**
Services Engineer: **Arup**
Project Manager: **Buro Four**

167

^ Exterior view
PAUL MCMULLIN

ALDHAM ROBARTS
LEARNING RESOURCE CENTRE

Maryland Street, Liverpool

Architect: Austin-Smith:Lord LLP
Construction Value: £8 million
Completion Date: 1993
Project Type: New-build and landscape renovation

Introduction

The Aldham Robarts Learning Resource Centre (LRC) at Liverpool John Moores University (formerly Liverpool Polytechnic) was probably the first of a new generation of university libraries in which computers and internet access were 'commingled' with book study. This process was known as 'SuperJANET' (Joint Academic NETwork), and was pioneered in the early 1990s.

One of the university's key objectives was for the architecture of the LRC to make a statement about the future of higher education in Liverpool. In addition, because of its position and pivotal role as a common resource, it was also intended to be a focal point for the academic community, replacing laboratory and lecture theatre as the learning hub of the institution.

Client's Brief

The brief inverted the traditional library ratio of book storage to study space, with a concept of 'commingling' IT and hard-copy use. The concept of silence in the reading room was also abandoned in favour of the buzz of industrious study.

In 1993, the recently formed Liverpool Polytechnic – later Liverpool John Moores University (LJMU) – constituted a coming-together of colleges (commerce, technology, art and teaching) with a collection of 'remaindered' municipal buildings spread across the city and suburbs, which represented outdated learning and accommodation strategies. As part of a wider drive to consolidate the new institution into three city-centre locations, new libraries or learning resource centres (LRCs) were required. At the same time, the 'Poly' needed a physical signifier to establish its presence and identity.

The Aldham Robarts Centre (LRC 1) brief was led by the Head of Library Services, Don Revill, and a senior architecture tutor, Geoff Hackman. Both shared a rare mix of vision and pragmatism. Significantly, Don's approach was revolutionary, if not 'heretical' in library circles. At the time, books were kept in libraries where silence reigned and computers were accessed at computing centres. The brief for ARC 1 was based on learning not reading: it was to be a place where books and computers were 'commingled', where group study was recognised and accommodated as part of project-based learning; where the librarian's first priority was coaching users, not keeping books. This enabled new technologies to be introduced and, in a profession where silence in libraries was mandatory, refocused on serious study. A decade and a half later, such activity is considered normal, but it was revolutionary at the time.

Design Process

There should be a place with great tables on which the librarian can put the books, and the reader should be able to take the book and go to the light

Louis Kahn, talking about his Phillips Exeter Academy Library

A glazed atrium faces the campus garden at the crossroads of pedestrian routes. In the atrium, floor levels are visually connected – allowing visitors to orientate themselves, while clearly seeing how the building works. A celebratory staircase, with two major cross-routes established at all levels, helps to organise the building. It spirals down from upper floors to the lower-ground level, and provides access to an enclosed bridge-link to the adjacent Aquinas Building. The 'Aquinas' was incorporated and adapted when policy changes during construction added a further library to the facility.

The four levels of the LRC are split into two zones: the upper floors contain book stacks and 'premium' quiet-study spaces; the ground floor and basement are characterised by noisier, more diverse activity – issue and return, group study and social areas.

The brief inverted the traditional library ratio of book storage to study space, with a concept of 'commingling' IT and hard-copy use.

Study spaces, in groups of four, are related to window openings within a perimeter zone. The deeper-plan areas accommodate either the book stacks or group-study spaces. Access floors and controllable artificial lighting ensure the complete interchangeability of book stacks, study tables and VDU-equipped workstations.

Concern that the 5,500 m² of space would dominate its surroundings resulted in the decision to use the external expression of the internal 'streets' to subdivide the main form of the building into four blocks. The natural slope of the site was used to create a lower-ground floor, with the ground around the building cut away in order to allow daylight to penetrate the double-height perimeter space which connects the ground and lower-ground floors.

Originally intended to replace a derelict church on Rodney Street (Liverpool's 'Harley Street'), the university was subsequently convinced that the setting and operational needs of the building dictated a larger site. Immediately behind the church, a tired gymnasium, no longer fit for purpose, presented the opportunity to formally relate to the shell of the church as a future expansion opportunity. The new site also sat within the large, wooded garden space of the Notre Dame Convent, which had been acquired by the polytechnic.

The Rodney Street Conservation Area is dominated by Liverpool's cathedrals and characterised by Georgian brick terraces of three and four storeys. The new building would have a footprint and bulk which was vastly larger than its neighbours. Contextual and figure ground studies, plus elevational study of the surrounding streets, therefore ran in parallel with development of the building's functional plan. The final layout, massing and elevations acknowledge the rhythms and texture of the areas without slavishly copying detail, form or material. As an accidental bonus, the organising atrium enjoys views of Gibberd's Roman Catholic cathedral towering over the convent buildings, and immediately axial to one of the cross-routes established within the building is the dominant bulk of Gilbert Scott's Anglican cathedral.

Project Evaluation

When opened, the first phase of the Aldham Robarts Learning Resource Centre, 'LRC 1', proved an immediate success, with over 2,500 reader visits per day. The following phase, 'LRC 2', was subsequently developed on the Liverpool John Moores University's 'City Campus'.

The university's Department for Construction developed and subsequently maintained a project-evaluation study of the Aldham Robarts Centre, both as a feedback device and as a learning tool.

The building is essentially adaptable. Whilst it appears to have a square plan, it is effectively an L-shaped building, served by an atrium space in the 'elbow' of the plan. The wings of the building are 15 m deep and planned to a 1.5 m module around a 'tartan' structural grid. Each bay is served by drop-down mechanical ventilation and lighting trays, integrated with the ceiling system: a sophisticated high-specification office solution, procured opportunistically when the market for office buildings suddenly collapsed during the detailed design of the centre. Consequently, glazed rooms have been erected

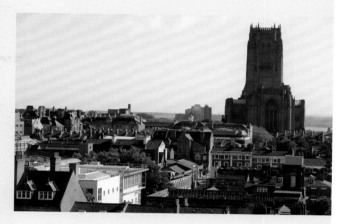

^ View of Aldham Robarts in its context
PAUL MCMULLIN

and dismantled during the life of the building, taking advantage of the high levels of daylight on each floor and the planned services infrastructure.

The careful, contextual design of the building made it possible to seamlessly connect the neighbouring Aquinas Building during the build phase. Subsequent designs for the derelict St Andrew's Church have further demonstrated the logical and obvious potential for connections which were incorporated in the design.

The ultimate success of this building lies in the singular engagement between the client and the designers at the outset of the project. Unencumbered by conflicting management concerns and committed unswervingly to realise a vision – to satisfy a perceived need with excellence – the building, which proved affordable both on completion and in use, transcends simple, operational requirements by developing a facility which is in every sense sustainable.

PROJECT TEAM

Client: **Liverpool John Moores University**
Architect: **Austin-Smith:Lord LLP**
Main Contractor: **Norwest Holst (Now Vinci)**
Quantity Surveyor: **Walfords (now Ridge)**
Structural Engineer: **Arup**
Services Engineer: **Arup**

The client was committed to
a highly sustainable building
that would reflect the ethos of
the academy and its particular
curriculum emphasis on
environmental issues.

^ Exterior view
MARTIN WORKMAN

ACADEMY OF
ST FRANCIS OF ASSISI

Gardners Drive, Liverpool

Architect: Capita Percy Thomas
Construction Value: £16.8 million
Completion Date: May 2006
Project Type: New-build

Introduction

The Academy of St Francis of Assisi is a new 900-place
City Academy in the economically deprived inner-
city area of Kensington in Liverpool. The academy's
specialism is the Environment, and this has been
reflected both in the building's design and in the
development of its curriculum. It was the highest rated
school in the UK in the recently published 'value-
added' league tables, and the teaching staff attest to a
dramatic improvement in the behaviour and well-being
of students since the opening of the new building.

The academy demonstrates how a large structure
with an intense use can be successfully designed
in a historically sensitive area, and how that context
can influence not just the building itself but the way
in which it is used. The particular specialism of the
curriculum – Environment – is perfectly matched by the
sensory environment of the public park, and the pupils'
awareness of the surroundings and the sustainability
merits of the institution are contributory factors in
its success. Whilst there was some criticism that the
academy had been constructed in a public park, the
site was actually a depot: unkempt and closed to the
public. The academy has opened up the area, not just
to staff and pupils but also to the local community, and
represents a positive addition to the park.

Client's Brief

The client's vision was for the academy to have a
strong Christian ethos without being a conventional
'faith' school. Accordingly, the design seeks to introduce
a setting which actively engages with the wider
community. The site for the academy is a former city-
council environmental depot on the edge of a Victorian
park, and the design strategy has been developed
to repair the urban and landscape fabric of an area
urgently requiring social and economic regeneration.

Though the area is deprived, the site is in a sensitive
setting, with attractive Victorian housing close to its
southern boundary. Advice from both Liverpool City
Council Planning Department and English Heritage
emphasised the need for the building design to
respond sympathetically to its delicate urban context.
The academy provides full facilities for 900 students,
ranging in age from 11 to 16 years old and drawn from
the immediately local community without the use of a
selection process.

The client was also committed to a highly sustainable
building that would reflect the ethos of the academy
and its particular curriculum emphasis on environmental
issues. In pre-application meetings with consultees, a
position was agreed that there would be no attempt to
try and hide or disguise the building in any way through
structural landscaping, but that it would make a positive
contribution to the Grade II registered Newsham Park.

Design Process

St Francis of Assisi is the first City Academy to
specialise in the Environment, and the client's
brief stressed the need for the building to facilitate
environmental education, to model good environmental-
design practice and, if possible, to offer itself as
an educational resource so that its environmental
strategies were clearly evident to the building users.
The building achieved an 'Excellent' rating in an
independent, preliminary BREEAM assessment.

The academy has an east–west orientation, designed to
maximise solar benefits, and simplify solar control, and
is on a number of levels: to the west, a courtyard space
is bounded by single- and two-storey buildings; while
a four-storey teaching block with a south-facing solar
atrium bounds the northern edge, with its classrooms
orientated to enjoy good views across the park. The
sports and assembly-hall spaces are built into a top-lit

basement, topped with an elevated outdoor classroom and wildflower garden. The project retained a number of historic buildings and adapted and reused these so that the frontage to the park remained intact. This allowed for continuity, and also captured the embedded energy in these existing buildings as part of a sustainable approach to the design process.

The building is concrete framed, using a flat-slab construction, with floor slabs and basement walls left exposed in order to give thermal-mass benefits; it is insulated considerably in excess of current Building Regulations standards. Its external walls are predominantly clad in Douglas Fir certified by the Forest Stewardship Council (FSC), with brickwork to low level on the north elevation, while the projecting bays are copper-clad. The 'glazing' to the solar atrium is ETFE transparent foil, with a dot-matrix fritting for thermal control. Louvres for natural ventilation are manually operated, involving the building users in the all-important process of choosing their own environmental conditions. A bank of 12 photovoltaic cells on the central spine of the building, clearly visible to pupils from the solar atrium, provides over ten per cent of the student-controlled energy requirements of the academy; the outputs from these, and the rainwater harvesting system, are prominently located on electronic display boards in the central cyber-café area.

The building's roofs are predominantly a combination of sedum and 'brown-roof' construction methods, with a substrate provided by sandstone excavated from the site; on the wildflower roof garden, crushed cockleshells have been added to the sandstone in order to provide a growing medium. The sedum roofs on the single-storey classroom wings for Years 7 and 8 trail down the north elevations to provide planted façades. External landscaped zones include garden areas specifically for pupils in Years 7 and 8. The materials – including the FSC Douglas Fir externally and internally, mineral wall paints, and recycled floor finishes and furniture laminates – have all been selected in order to minimise their impact on the environment.

Project Evaluation

The constraints of the tight site – bounded between a historic park to the north, residential properties close to the southern boundary and existing historic buildings to the west – offered opportunities to explore imaginative design solutions relevant to the specificities of the location. Lowering the hall spaces into a basement level; stacking teaching spaces over four storeys, with views over the park and connected by a solar atrium; and forming a domestically scaled courtyard in order to create a sensitive connection with the existing buildings give the academy a strong and distinctive personality. In post-occupancy discussions with students, it was apparent that the spatial delight that these spaces provide is as vital for improved educational outcomes as the functional provision of appropriate learning facilities.

The restricted site also created a challenge in terms of the provision of adequate external spaces. In response, the design utilises opportunities for creating as much diversity as possible in order to use external spaces

^^ Photovoltaic panels on the roof
PAUL MCMULLIN

^ Internal corridor
PAUL MCMULLIN

creatively: the roof over the hall spaces provides an outdoor learning environment and cultivation area, whilst small 'back gardens' are provided immediately outside classrooms for Year 7 students to develop with their chosen planting schemes. Careful negotiations with local community groups have overcome initial scepticism, to enable the adjacent under-utilised park to provide grass sports pitches for the academy.

PROJECT TEAM

Client: **Department for Education and Skills (DfES)/Diocese and Archdiocese of Liverpool**
Architect: **Capita Percy Thomas**
Quantity Surveyor: **Gardiner & Theobald**
M&E Engineer: **Buro Happold**
Services Engineer: **Buro Happold**
Project Manager: **Turner & Townsend**
Landscape Architect: **Fira Landscape**
Acoustic Engineer: **Buro Happold**
Environmental Design Consultant: **Buro Happold**

4
SHAPING THE FUTURE

Are successful cities snapshots or cumulative historical documentaries? Are they fixed or fluid? Single path or layered? Living or dead?

Venice is an exquisite example of a beautiful urban corpse. But then New York and Paris are, to be honest, also identified in our imaginations with a single historical period. Surely there is no question that Manhattan's heroic architectural age had a beginning and end whose dates were circa 1920 and circa 1980? Our idea of Paris (at least, some 60 per cent of it) was determined by Baron Haussmann during a busy life which ended in 1891.

< Liverpool as seen from the Hope Street Hotel
PAUL MCMULLIN

The twentieth century did not serve Liverpool well. Compared to the extraordinary growth and optimism the city experienced between 1750 and 1900 and the fantastic legacy of buildings it left behind, the past century has been a melancholy catalogue of destruction and neglect. There are some splendid exceptions to that sad judgement, but until very recently it was difficult to include the words 'Liverpool' and 'future' in the same sentence.

Liverpool One may not have the same consistent style or dirigiste certainties of Haussmann, but the development boldly reinvents the city centre and its design won for BDP a Stirling Prize nomination in 2009, the first time such a distinction has been awarded to a masterplan. And while Haussmann has his critics for destroying Paris' medieval heart, Liverpool One destroyed little of value while replacing the tired and redundant with energy and enthusiasm. There have been critics who cite a facile commercial Esperanto, but these critics do not perhaps remember how dire Lord Street was in 1972. It's an enthusiastic start to that extraordinary challenge of reviving a city.

So what next? Liverpool's famous architecture was an expression of unique historic circumstances. It would be idle to anticipate a stimulating repetition of them. We are not going to have Irish merchants building a new Rodney Street, nor ambitious civic dignitaries another St George's Hall. Even Liverpool cannot cope, one imagines, with another cathedral. And the maritime economy whose pilots created the splendid *rus in urbe* of Sefton Park has disappeared.

But the reason to know history is so as not to repeat it. New sources of wealth in education and brain-led businesses will make their own architectural demands. Liverpool still has many problems, but the assets of culture, site and spirit are more valuable than the liability of a hesitant economy. Powerful and confident new buildings are the evidence of Liverpool's past.

The same must be said of Liverpool's future. The city has been revived: now it must live.

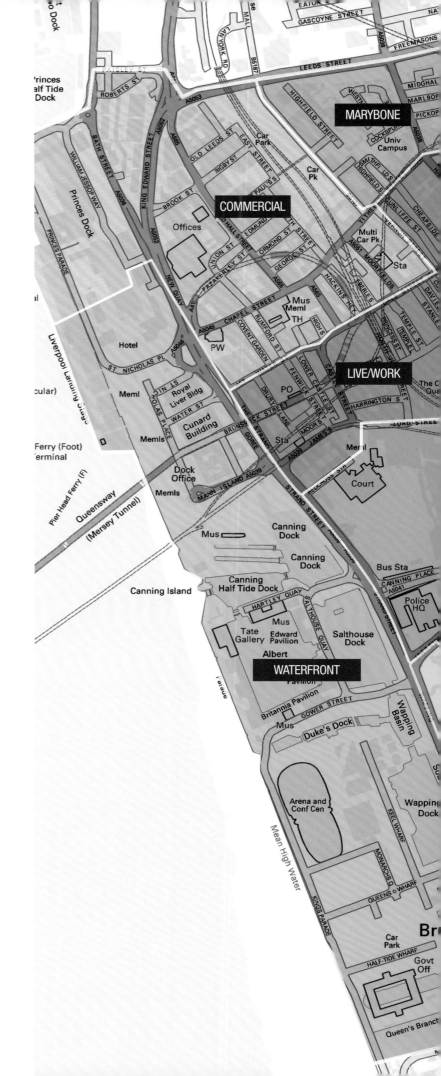

174

> Illustration showing development zones, Liverpool

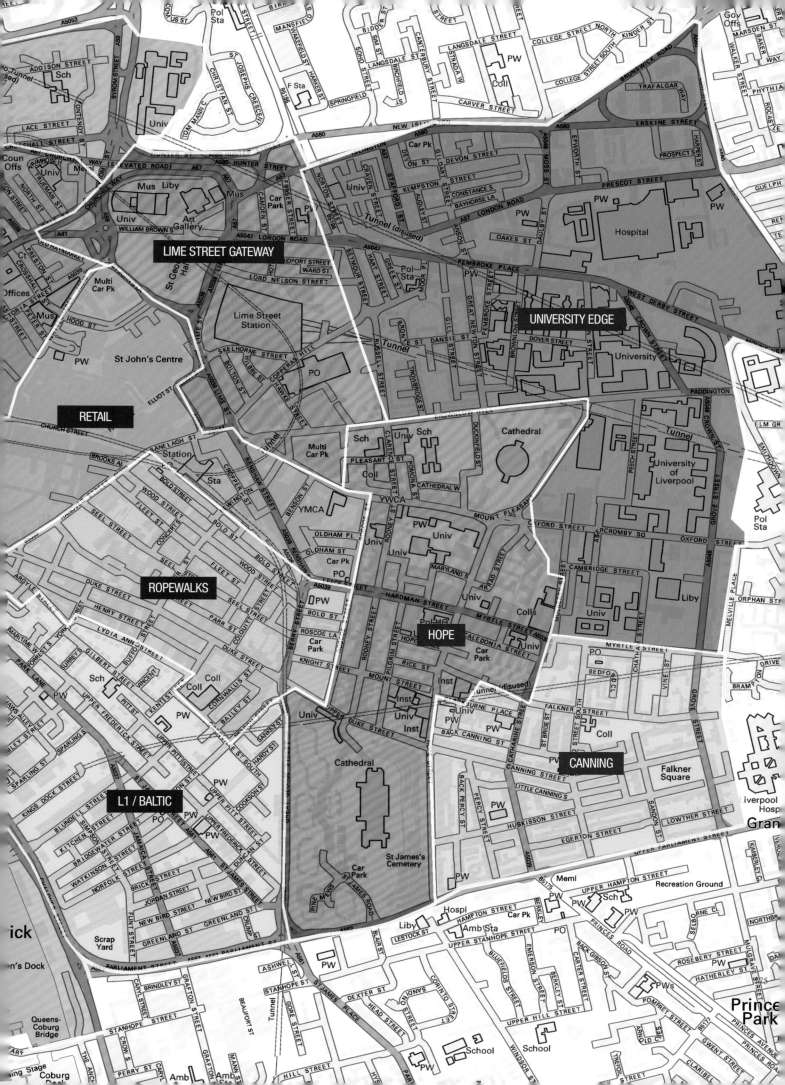

OPEN FOR BUSINESS

There is something about Liverpool. It is inspiring and challenging in equal measures, a self-deprecating and proud city. Its people are passionate about the place, more so than any other city I know. This passion has served Liverpool well in the past and left a unique legacy in the built environment, its culture and the character of its people. In a shrinking world, with globalisation producing both opportunity and loss, these are important imprints. The DNA of Liverpool is comprised of imagination, invention and adaptability.

Liverpool has always been a city of commerce, with a smaller manufacturing base than other cities. It is crucial that the city retains manufacturing as a means of employment – particularly its cluster of life science industry – at the same time as boosting our commercial activity in digital, culture and other sectors. The success and growth of tourism and a huge improvement in our retail offer have transformed the city's image and attractiveness.

Along with investment in infrastructure and capital developments, the city will continue to up-skill its workforce and progress educational achievements. Improvements in our numerous great parks and the range of housing are crucial if we are to retain and increase our population and wealth.

The city centre is a much more attractive place than it was and investors have not been slow to recognise further potential. In particular, Liverpool's monumental waterfront will change dramatically over the next few decades. With a complete attitudinal shift in approach and expectation, Liverpool is now used to demanding the best and highest quality with its new developments.

The confidence at home has grown terrifically in the last ten years with the city looking outwards again to seek new partners in trade, culture and friendship. Liverpool is always open to new ideas and will be pursuing the best ways of enjoying our heritage to drive new economic progress and create a greener, more sustainable city for future generations.

John Kelly
Executive Director for Regeneration
Liverpool City Council

JOHN KELLY

John Kelly, Executive Director for Regeneration at Liverpool City Council, has worked on most of the city's large regeneration projects including the successful bid to be European Capital of Culture in 2008, creating a new Science Park company with the city's two universities, and setting up Liverpool Vision. He has responsibility for economic development, tourism, culture, transportation, planning and the Council's assets.

Prior to his nine years with the City Council, he worked for the Regional Development Agency and for Central Government on Urban Regeneration for 15 years. He has also worked as a licensed croupier and building site labourer.

MAKE NO LITTLE PLANS –
BLUEPRINT FOR SUCCESS

In 2000 a former colleague at Liverpool Vision, Graham Marshall, our first Planning Director, described Liverpool as a baggy jumper. Without taking the analogy too far, he was describing a city that had been built for over one million people and was occupied by less than 500,000. The city centre (aka baggy jumper) was under occupied and full of holes (some of them dating back as far as the Second World War bomb damage). Over time I have increasingly appreciated the aptness of what, at the time, seemed rather a bizarre analogy.

The last 10 years have seen those holes filled and effectively stitched back into the fabric of the city, with an emphatic emphasis on place-making and connectivity. Liverpool One epitomises this – a development which has slipped seamlessly, but with much aplomb, into the city, reconnecting areas that had previously functioned in isolation. The fact that BDP's masterplan was shortlisted for the Stirling Prize in 2009 and that at the time of writing, Christmas 2009, its shops and restaurants are allegedly exceeding trading figures across the UK, bears testament to the fact that if you get the place-making right, the people will come ... and they will spend. Liverpool's renaissance has been founded on a range of factors but there can be no doubting the pivotal role Liverpool One has played in the story. I was involved at the beginning when Liverpool set down a marker, making clear to somewhat bemused developers and investors wedded to out-of-town mall developments that we wanted 'streets for people'. Grosvenor understood our vision and it is enormously rewarding to witness the impact the development has had and the way the people have almost instantaneously populated it, so there is a seamless join between the traditional heart of the main retail area and its new 'extension'.

Moving forward, I am hopeful that Liverpool will continue to be in the vanguard, ensuring that the places we create will be for the people who will inhabit them as much as for the developers and investors who will finance them. Whether it be continued development of our waterfront at Kings Dock, the expansion of our commercial district or the ambitious proposals for Liverpool Waters, architects and designers working in Liverpool will continue to ensure that they stitch those holes in the jumper back together seamlessly as the city expands to fill out. The challenge will not be around the form of development – we have learnt those lessons well – it will be ensuring that the new-found economic well-being captures and benefits the whole community, particularly those in north Liverpool where economic and social deprivation remain at unacceptably high levels.

One of the most fascinating parts of place-making is watching how people move around and use spaces when they are developed. An army of ants moving into areas previously blocked off, finding new ways around their territory. In Liverpool, where the interventions and public realm improvements have had an impact all over the city centre, the effect is particularly evident. New mental maps are being created and people are finding themselves walking through areas they had never visited before. Long may it continue – Liverpool is a walkable city and we must ensure it continues to be.

The future for Liverpool in terms of its physical fabric looks promising; an unrivalled legacy of 19th and early 20th-century buildings, a World Heritage Site and an increasingly confident understanding of place-making for the 21st Century. If there is a challenge for the development industry it is ensuring that sustainability and the environmental agenda are firmly embedded in our thinking, whether it be in the detail of individual buildings and spaces or via larger interventions in our infrastructure.

With the increased confidence that the last 10 years have brought the city, we now seem ready to return our sights to the international stage. It is well documented that Liverpool's 19th and early 20th-century growth was founded on international trade, and although some of that trade was unforgiveable, there are more laudable aspects of the psyche that drove that growth that are re-emerging. Outward looking, more US than UK, entrepreneurial and independent; England is our backyard and our eyes are turning to the world in front of us again.

Jenny Douglas
Head of City Centre and Urban Design
Liverpool Vision

JENNY DOUGLAS

Jenny Douglas leads on the physical and economic regeneration of Liverpool City Centre for Liverpool Vision, the city's Economic Development Agency. Originally qualifying as a Town Planner, she has based her career in Liverpool working for both the City Council and Liverpool Vision in a variety of areas covering Planning, Development and Urban Design.

Liverpool Vision was established as the city's Economic Development Agency in 2008, bringing together Liverpool Vision (Economic Development Agency) with a focus on the city centre, the council's economic development arm, Business Liverpool, and Liverpool Land Development Company, which focused primarily on development in the Speke/Garston and Edge Lane areas of the city. The company is now focused on facilitating and bringing forward the city's global / internationalisation agenda and enterprise, business support and physical development activity across the city. Priorities include north Liverpool, continued investment in the development of the city centre and a drive to increase business start ups, business growth and inward investment. Primarily Liverpool Vision is a facilitator, an organisation with an unrivalled reputation within the development and business communities for making things happen.

BEYOND THE OBVIOUS

As a teenager I had a Saturday job in a shop on Bold Street. The city centre became a playground. The narrow streets and abandoned warehouses of Ropewalks provided bars and clubs to discover and the faded grandeur of Canning and Hope Street a bohemian crowd of new friends. The exhilaration of these adolescent experiences has long since dimmed but a staff Christmas meal in the suburbs sticks in the memory and has coloured the way I have thought about Liverpool ever since.

To get to the restaurant, in a former palatial mercantile residence overlooking Sefton Park, we travelled the two-thirds of a mile length of Princes Avenue: the grand processional route designed by Joseph Paxton to link his Princes Park with what were the outermost reaches of the city centre in the 1840s. The carriageways and central green ribbon are held by imposing 19th-century terraces punctuated by an outstanding collection of religious buildings from the Byzantine domes of the Greek Orthodox Church of St Nicholas to the Moorish turrets of the synagogue. On either side of the main avenue, tree-lined streets of more modest houses step away into the distance before it culminates in the great iron gates of the Park. Here unfolded a city of genuine scale and substance with a depth of character far beyond the obvious delights of its centre.

The phenomenal wealth and confidence that fashioned Liverpool's renowned waterfront and city centre also created rich and varied townscapes in the inner suburbs. Just as the exuberant banks, exchanges and insurance houses of the commercial district sit back-to-back with robust yet characterful warehouses, so elaborate Victorian villas neighbour streets of solid bylaw housing in areas like Toxteth, Wavertree and Fairfield. Here too there is fine civic and commercial architecture, albeit of a more modest nature, and expansive 19th-century parks. These are highly distinctive places that should be viewed as some of Liverpool's greatest assets. The next great challenge is to apply the experience gained from the remarkable transformation of the city centre to its less appreciated residential hinterland. Liverpool has to learn to love its suburbs once again.

Liverpool needs more people. If the city is to retain its population and attract new inhabitants it must ensure that there are attractive places to live, and where better than within walking distance of the city centre? Fortunately much of it is already in place. Unfortunately, like the Albert Dock and Ropewalks decades earlier, its value is yet to be fully realised. A coherent, long-term vision is required to raise aspirations and unlock the true potential of the inner suburbs. This must be based upon these areas' inherent assets rather than importing stock solutions from elsewhere. Buildings and spaces need to be re-used in a sustainable manner, the damaged urban fabric knitted back together and the consequences of past clearance programmes viewed as exciting opportunities to create new neighbourhoods that delight and inspire.

As has happened time and time again in the city centre, there needs to be a clear break with the established orthodoxy. Risks will have to be taken. Difficulties will be compounded by the lack of the sort of public resources that underpinned much of the recent redevelopment. Considered planning, enlightened developers, entrepreneurial acumen and skilful design need to reach beyond the inner ring road. As this publication hopefully illustrates Liverpool has always been at its best when rising to a challenge and demanding solutions worthy of a great city.

John Stonard
CABE Programme Manager
Design Liverpool

JOHN STONARD

John Stonard manages Design Liverpool, a CABE Regional Pilot developed in partnership with Liverpool City Council, Liverpool Vision and Places Matter. The aim of the project is to explore how national objectives for promoting excellence in the built environment can be promoted at a local level through a combination of skills development, enabling and advocacy.

Brought up 'over the water' in Birkenhead, John initially trained as a landscape architect before pursuing further studies in town planning and urban design. Having worked for a number of architectural practices and public agencies within the north of England he spent three years managing the Historic Environment of Liverpool Project for English Heritage before taking his current position in 2005.

'WE'D HAVE TO INVENT IT!'

I escaped here from the Isle of Man. Clever boys went to Liverpool University. Really clever boys went to Oxbridge. So I came to Liverpool. I count myself charmed that I never really ever left, even if sometimes I went away. I think I am now an honorary Scouser. I arrived in October 1962 – just months before the Beatles put Liverpool on the map. Perhaps that's why I innocently tried to pick up John's wife in the Cavern while he was on stage singing. I've still got the psychological bruises from her response. But it goes to show you always learn something in Liverpool. And yes, to be there then was very heavenly – almost as good as it is now.

Liverpool is endlessly difficult and fascinating. You'd never invent it. But it retains its iron grip on our imagination. And the city has been good to me. It made me an 'expert' on cities. I first wrote about its political, financial and economic travails in the 1980s – *Liverpool on the Brink. Drink* to my friends. I thought, if I can get this story right I can write about anywhere. It's amazing how far and how quickly the city has come on since then, especially during the last five years. And it's never going back to where it was – even if it slips a little from time to time. You can just tell. But Scousers are self aware. They know they fell a long way down. And they know they're nearer the beginning than the end of their long and winding road back.

I know no other city where the people, place, architecture, language and culture merge and morph so easily and endlessly. And I don't need to quote the numbers of listed buildings. I live in a Victorian house in Toxteth and work in a Georgian merchant's house in Rodney Street. From there I can see a mock Gothic and a Modernist cathedral, McCartney's Liverpool Institute for Performing Arts (LIPA), the fabulous new Liverpool One – all set against Jesse Hartley's Albert Dock masterpiece and the widest river and highest sky I know. Some don't like Liverpool's new buildings. I do. I love them. In fact I'd give Rod Holmes of Grosvenor Estates a Knighthood for creating a place fit for Scousers. But it doesn't really matter if you don't like the new buildings. Mere stones couldn't crush the Scouser spirit.

This is supposed to be about Future Visions for Liverpool. As an urban 'expert' I should now quote my professional mantra about what makes a successful European city – innovation, diversity, connectivity, place quality, good governance. And I should ask how well Liverpool is doing and what else it should do to do better. If I were to answer, I would say – coming along. But more work is required.

But I save my answers for other cities. Liverpool does not need any wisdom I might have about successful places. It's where I learnt it. My messages are not necessary in Liverpool. They're in its DNA. Even if they haven't always done it, Scousers know what they have to do to make a proper place.

My vision of Liverpool's future is simple. Actually, it's a cliché. The city must and will be what it always has been – true to its persistently aggravating, cosmopolitan, self-regarding, expansive self. There will be ups and downs. Economic crashes – and buildings – will come and go. But Liverpool will always be the same. Big hearted. Open minded. Querulous. Slightly surreal. It will always attract the curious and the interesting. They will never know where the story is going. That's why they come. That's why it will always be there. Perhaps we would invent it.

Professor Michael Parkinson CBE,
Director, European Institute for urban Affairs
Liverpool John Moores University

PROFESSOR MICHAEL PARKINSON CBE

Michael is Director of the European Institute for Urban Affairs at Liverpool John Moores University. He recently completed for the government *The Credit Crunch and Regeneration: Impact and Implications*. He produced the *State of the English Cities* Report in 2006 for the Office of the Deputy Prime Minister – the authoritative analysis of cities in Britain. He leads the Department of Communities and Local Government's expert panel on Regeneration and Economic Development Analysis. He was Director of the ESRC's Programme on CITIES: Cohesion and Competitiveness, a major five-year research programme involving 25 Universities.

Michael has acted as adviser on urban affairs to the European Commission, OECD, EUROCITIES, the Department of Communities and Local Government, the National Audit Office, the House of Commons Select Committees, the Core Cities and a range of cities in the UK. He lectures extensively nationally and internationally and is a regular contributor to the media.

LIVERPOOL – GLOBAL CITY?

I came to Merseyside over 20 years ago, at a time when everyone else seemed to be going in the other direction. Although I am passionate about my adopted city, my first impressions were far from positive. How had Liverpool allowed itself to become so fractured? And more importantly, how could it possibly recover and repair itself? There appeared to be no hope, no plan A for recovery, let alone a plan B. The glass was neither half full nor half empty, there simply was no glass.

But if cities are organisms, then the potential for self-cure must remain, albeit aided by judicious and timely medication. Liverpool is once again in rude health, there is a buzz about the place that emanates not from flies circling a cadaver, but a new self-belief and confidence. This is a city that knows it can achieve. The old sickness occasionally shows itself, to remind Liverpool that although recovery is strong, it is remission and not a permanent cure.

Yet Liverpool has shown that its heart and vital organs function as they should. Nurturing and care are required. Cosmetic surgery alone will not cure all the sickness – it simply disguises the symptoms. It may seem anathema to many architects and urban designers, who believe their skills to be a panacea, but improving the built environment is only one approach, and will only prevail as part of a holistic approach to treatment.

Good design has certainly helped in recent years. Liverpool One is an exemplar scheme and is fast becoming a model of good practice in using large scale, mixed use development that helps stitch the city centre back together. The waterfront developments at Pier Head and the Arena illustrate how to design in an unashamedly contemporary manner and complement a sensitive historic environment. Context is the starting point for the design process, and this must continue if Liverpool is to complete its renaissance and return to being a global city. Whilst this may seem an unrealistic ambition, it is not a new status for the city, for Liverpool has already enjoyed this position. It is simply recognition of potential, and a belief in quality.

The transformation of the city centre in recent years needs to be matched in other areas, most notably north Liverpool. At the time of writing, a strategic regeneration framework for this area is in preparation, in addition to an emerging masterplan for the waterfront to the north of the city centre. Both offer synergies and exciting prospects for the city as a whole, and a solution to the question that I asked myself 20 years ago – how can the city repair itself? For now the city must keep taking the tablets, but its eventual cure is in its own hands, and self-belief is a powerful medicine. And Liverpool is not short of self-belief.

Rob Burns
Urban Design Manager
Liverpool City Council

ROB BURNS

Rob is Urban Design Manager for the City Council, and has lived in Merseyside for over 20 years. Rob started his career as an archaeologist working in the UK and later in North Africa and the Middle East, as a UNESCO consultant, before moving into the historic built environment as a local authority conservation officer. Working with English Heritage as a Historic Areas Advisor in the north west of England, Rob has been directly involved with the major regeneration projects in Liverpool since the late 1990's, and this has continued in his current role.

He is a panel member for the regional design review Places Matter! and has given presentations on urban design and the regeneration of Liverpool in many places ranging from Shanghai to Stavanger, as well as advising the Geddes Institute on the future of Scottish cities.

L1 (MARK 2)

In *Notes from a Small Island*, Bill Bryson comments on his arrival at Liverpool Lime Street, that the city was hosting 'a festival of litter.' For me, what this observation summed up was a lack of pride in this once grand city – by those responsible for the urban realm rather than, the people of Liverpool. Years of bad planning, traffic-focused interventions and general neglect had left a run-down, fragmented city centre. This is the city I remember leaving at the age of 18.

Fortunately, the last ten years have been kind to Liverpool. One catalyst in the changing attitude to the industrial northern city came from developers Urban Splash who appreciated the raw quality of the warehouses and old buildings of Liverpool. They created new homes and social spaces in the middle of the city for a young tribe of urbanites. But, most importantly, they brought new life to the city centre and started to create a new image for Liverpool – as a vibrant, cosmopolitan city of clubs, cafes and culture.

Finally, ambitions were raised and investment and development was encouraged. What has resulted is a mixture of projects of varied quality that have begun the process of remaking the city. On a large scale it is the huge shopping development, Liverpool One, which sets the standard for what can be achieved. It has created a new city quarter of high quality with buildings and streetscapes by some leading UK architects and designers.

I was delighted to have the chance to build in my home city with Unity – a housing and office scheme built as a new landmark to symbolise the regeneration of the city. It references Liverpool's and my own personal history. The elevations were inspired by the Dazzle Ship patterns created by the World War I vorticists painted in Liverpool's docks. The façade also spells out my mum's name in Morse code down the front.

With the financial downturn, the city has time to assess what has been achieved and plan strategically for the next wave of development. This needs to carefully knit together the often disparate and incoherent buildings created in the boom with the fine commercial grain of the Victorian city. But there are two areas of Liverpool that need to be given considerable thought: the quarter bordered by Lime Street/Church Street/ Whitechapel and the waterfront.

The area South of Lime Street has great potential – it is a transport hub with a large shopping centre, several grand department stores, two theatres, the iconic Tower Restaurant and Williamson Square. It is a natural heart to the city; however, Liverpool One has changed the commercial centre of gravity and the quarter has now fallen into neglect. A strong and inventive vision is required.

Similarly, the historic waterfront needs to be seen as a whole landscape where new additions such as the Museum of Liverpool and the Liverpool Echo Arena are creatively connected to more established landmarks like Albert Dock. Poor quality developments, like Princess Dock, show precisely how not to develop the amazing potential of the riverfront. Again, a powerful vision and stronger guidelines are needed to take up this challenge.

Liverpool is becoming a great city and has a number of exemplary projects that set the standard for future work. The task is now to build on this at a large and small scale, and use the great local talent too often overlooked. It is only in this way that Liverpool will create its own indigenous urban identity.

Paul Monaghan
Partner
Allford Hall Monaghan Morris Architects

PAUL MONAGHAN

Paul is a co-founding Partner of Allford Hall Monaghan Morris, a leading architectural practice in London. He is involved in the design, development and review stages of projects, and influences the strategic direction of the practice. He played a major role in the development Westminster Academy which has won over 15 prestigious design awards including best school, best public building and best London Building.

In 2000 he joined the CABE Enabling Panel and in 2008 he became Vice Chair of the CABE Schools Design Review Panel, identifying and reviewing design quality within the entire Building Schools for the Future Programme.

Paul has been chairman of the Young Architect of the Year award and he is currently a judge for the RIBA Awards Panel which presides over the Stirling Prize.

FURTHER READING

Fleetwood-Hesketh, P *Murray's Lancashire Architectural Guide* (J. Murray, 1955).

Hignett, S *A Picture to Hang on the Wall* (Joseph, 1966).

Hughes, Q *Liverpool – city of architecture* (Bluecoat Press, 1999).

Hughes, Q *Seaport, architecture and townscape in Liverpool* (Lund Humphries, 1964).

McGough, R et al. *Penguin Modern Poets : The Mersey Sound* (Penguin, 1967).

du Noyer, P *Liverpool : wondrous place, music from Cavern to Cream* (Virgin, 2002).

Pevsner, N *South Lancashire* (Pevsner Architectural Guides: Buildings of England) (Yale Universty Press, 1969).

Picton, J A *Architectural History of Liverpool* (1858).

Picton, J A *Memorials of Liverpool: historical and topographical, including a history of the dock estate. – Vol.1 Historical, Vol 2 Topographical* (Gilbert G. Walmsley, 1903)

Rickman, T *An Attempt to Discriminate the Styles of English Architecture from the Conquest to the Reformation* (1817).

Sharples, J *Liverpool* (Pevsner Architectural Guides: City Guides, 2004).

Turner, S *A Hard day's Write – the stories behind every Beatles' Song* (Little, Brown/ Carlton, 1994).

Willett, J *Art in a City* (published for the Bluecoat Society of Arts by Methuen, 1967).

Many further books, booklets and pamphlets are available from Liverpool Central Library (www.liverpool.gov.uk)